Parenting

while

Working

from

Home

Parenting
while
Working
from
Home

A Monthly Guide to Help Parents
Balance Their Careers
Connect with Their Kids
Establish Their Inner Strength

SHARI MEDINI & KARISSA TUNIS

Owners of AdoreThemParenting.com

Skyhorse Publishing

Copyright © 2021, 2023 by Shari Medini & Karissa Tunis

All rights reserved. No part of this book may be reproduced in any manner without the express written consent of the publisher, except in the case of brief excerpts in critical reviews or articles. All inquiries should be addressed to Skyhorse Publishing, 307 West 36th Street, 11th Floor, New York, NY 10018.

Skyhorse Publishing books may be purchased in bulk at special discounts for sales promotion, corporate gifts, fund-raising, or educational purposes. Special editions can also be created to specifications. For details, contact the Special Sales Department, Skyhorse Publishing, 307 West 36th Street, 11th Floor, New York, NY 10018 or info@skyhorsepublishing.com.

Skyhorse® and Skyhorse Publishing® are registered trademarks of Skyhorse Publishing, Inc.®, a Delaware corporation.

Visit our website at www.skyhorsepublishing.com.

10 9 8 7 6 5 4 3 2 1

Library of Congress Cataloging-in-Publication Data is available on file.

Cover design by Daniel Brount

Hardcover ISBN: 978-1-5107-6482-8
Paperback ISBN: 978-1-5107-7582-4
Ebook ISBN: 978-1-5107-6483-5

Printed in China

We dedicate this book to our supportive husbands and our amazing children.
Thank you for sharing this wonderful journey with us and for inspiring us to write about it.

Table of Contents

Introduction

Where do we even begin? Parents do it all.

We change dirty diapers. We chase little ones around at the playground. We prepare our growing kids for their first day of school. We wipe away tears and try to replace them with a smile. We bandage skinned knees and always keep ice packs in the freezer. We schedule, host, and referee playdates. We throw personalized birthday parties even when the requested theme isn't sold in stores. We pour bowls of cereal, pack lunches, cook dinners, and serve bedtime snacks. We help with the mind-boggling math homework. We cheer on our athletes from the sidelines. We take on the role of driving instructor and accept the gray hairs that come along with the process. We help our babies settle into college with a smile on our face, despite the emotions inside our heart.

From the moment our kids are born, we parent. We are there day in and day out, putting one foot in front of the other, just trying to do our best for our precious families. And on top of all of this? We are trying to advance in our careers while working from home.

Some days will be better than others. We totally get it! As fellow work-from-home parents with six kids between us, we are also trying to manage it all. Parenthood can be beautiful, complicated, emotional, and downright shocking. So it's no wonder that we can feel totally frustrated one moment and utterly grateful the next.

The ups and downs of parenthood are normal. However, we believe that the overall experience of parenting while working from home should be a positive one! There should be more good days than bad days. And we should be able to genuinely enjoy the time that we spend with our families while still being productive and managing our careers.

Parenting looks different in different seasons. When we embrace the fact that not every day, week, or month will be the same, we can begin to find more joy in the moment. As we move through the year, it's important to recognize how parenting strategies need to shift in order to create homes that are happy and kids who are thriving. This book encourages you to create space for new goals, activities, and experiences that will help you establish your inner strength, connect with your kids, and balance your career.

*

What You'll Find in This Book

December parenting is very different from July parenting. We could throw out any month of the year, and you would automatically think of a few seasonal challenges that come up in your household during those thirty days. Between holidays, school semesters, work commitments, sports, and other seasonal activities, each month is a little different. Throughout this book, we'll help you manage your workload month by month with practical tips, genuine encouragement, and proven strategies for intentional parenting and increased productivity. You'll be able to read about a new concept and begin implementing it that same afternoon.

We fully understand that it takes work to get to a better place! There is a need for reflection, planning, and learning to create a happier self, a happier family, and a happier home overall. But we know that you can get there . . . because we have taken this same journey ourselves. Month by month you can make small changes—both for yourself and your family. And by the end of this year, you'll be able to look back and appreciate how far you've come.

How This Book Is Organized

This book is laid out so that you can start reading it in January and use it as a guide over the course of a full year. However, if you pick it up during another month, you can simply jump to that chapter and use the book as a reference guide for the season you're in. The journal prompts for each month are intended to help you plan and grow over the course of the year as well.

Each month you will discover practical and positive tips to help you feel less overwhelmed, grow closer with your family, and overcome the challenges of working from home. You'll find great reminders for things you may have already known, and new a-ha moments for things you'd like to try. We know that each family is unique in its own way. What works for one parent won't work for another. But we hope that you find the inspiration and courage to try something new and seek a solution that works for your household.

In order to address the various aspects of family life, each chapter is divided into a few sections:

Focus on You

When you are doing well, the whole family functions even better. Which is exactly why we dedicate a section in each chapter to you. We cover topics like self-advocacy, time management, self-care, finding balance, self-confidence, and much more. Our goal is to help you find fulfillment in everyday life so that you can enjoy those precious moments with your family and meet your true potential in your career.

Connect with Your Kids

As parents, we spend a lot of time with our kids. This is a blessing, but it is also a challenge! How do you fill those hours, how do you make that time meaningful, and how do you continually enjoy each other's company? We share our favorite tips and tricks for spending lots (and lots) of time with your kids. Discover new activity ideas throughout the year, as well as parenting strategies to help your kids get along with friends, siblings, and, of course, you.

Work from Home

Raising children requires so much of our attention that maintaining a career amidst a chaotic environment can feel impossible. We have been there, but over the past decade of working from home, we have been able to find better ways to balance the demands. Learn how to set up your home in a way that works for you, your work, and your kids. Discover strategies to maintain your productivity, communicate professionally, build your network, and find ways to manage your time so that your work and your kids both get the attention that they need.

Reflect and Plan

Since we will be sharing a lot of information with you each month, we want to give you time and space to make the most of what you've learned. At the beginning and end of each chapter, you'll find Monthly Intentions and Monthly Reflections. These journaling prompts give you an opportunity to gather your thoughts from the previous month, and focus on a plan as you move forward into the next one.

*

Create Lasting Change

This book was born out of a realization that, like many other parents, we had been stuck in a cycle of consuming negative media. At first it can be humorous and comforting to know that you are not the only parent out there who is struggling; sometimes it helps to commiserate and joke about hiding in the bathroom with a bar of chocolate. However, when you're reading article after article where the author is complaining about their kids, their spouses, their messy houses, and their demanding bosses, you start to see your own life through that lens.

You get annoyed when your toddler spills their snack, instead of chuckling and realizing that that's what toddlers do. You get mad when your spouse leaves their toothbrush out, instead of realizing that it was because they were in a rush to get to work after they fed the kids breakfast that morning. You start to think that if you had a nicer house, your life would magically be more organized. And you begin to blame the workload assigned to you, instead of evaluating your own productivity.

This type of content has a "parents versus the world" message that can seem helpful on the surface. However, for us, it ended up creating more of a "parent versus their family" struggle when it came to daily life. These parenting articles were moving us further away from what we wanted most—a family that works together to build a happy life!

As a first step, we made the purposeful decision to stop consuming all of the negative parenting content. It was amazing how quickly we started to see a positive shift in our own lives. We found ourselves feeling happier and more energetic as parents, which then meant that our kids were happier and more pleasant to be around. That led to a cleaner and more organized house because we were once again respecting and appreciating our space. And when the home was calmer and cleaner, it became easier to stay focused on our careers. It snowballed quickly, and we began to feel empowered.

Day by day, month by month, we were able to make lasting changes. We found strategies that worked well for us and began sharing those positive, practical tips with our close friends. The most important lesson we learned was that there was nothing too big or too small to troubleshoot! If something was frustrating us, we could likely brainstorm a way to improve it.

Shortly after our own personal transformations began, we decided to collaborate on a new project: a parenting website. The plan for AdoreThemParenting.com was created on a cozy couch while our children played at our feet. What started out as a simple parenting website aimed to share our tips with friends and family quickly grew into something more.

We feel fortunate to have now collaborated with over one hundred experts that have weighed in on popular parenting topics. We have shared hundreds of articles and thousands of ideas in beautiful, encouraging ways. And we truly appreciate the opportunities we've had to inspire parents, grandparents, educators, and childcare providers around the globe.

Free Resources

Since we live in such a digital world, we want to offer you further resources on our website. These certainly aren't necessary for your book-reading experience. However, we have compiled some helpful parenting resources on our site that you are welcome to explore. You'll find notes throughout the book that will point you to free printables, kid activity ideas, family planners, and more. You can also connect with us anytime directly through our website. We always love hearing new ideas and stories from fellow parents! Simply go to our website: AdoreThemParenting.com/Book-Resources.

*

You Got This!

With the right strategies, you can create a more positive environment for everyone in your home. We have seen it in our own lives, and we have heard it from those in our parenting community. Since our children are only young once, we need to take action while we still have the chance. Thankfully, there are ways to make life feel more manageable so that you can enjoy those incredible little individuals that you tuck into bed every night.

You deserve to be happy, and so do they! While we can't promise that it will all be easy, we are excited for you to jump into this new chapter of parenting. Here's to shared struggles, new solutions, and calmer days ahead.

Sending you warm wishes and all our support,
Karissa & Shari

Chapter 1
January

At the start of the new year, we are all trying to find a balance between recovering from the holidays and preparing for the year ahead. This chapter encourages you to focus on yourself so that you can be more present for your family. We provide fun activity ideas that will help your kids with goal setting and communication. And we talk through the realities of working from home and the need to find a new balance.

*

Monthly Intentions

At the beginning of each month, we'll leave space for you to prioritize, plan, and prepare. As parents, our lives can start to feel like a series of small emergencies. One simple way to keep things organized is to set clear priorities and plan accordingly for the month ahead. Answering these five questions at the start of each month only takes a few minutes, but it will help you feel organized and ready to tackle the next thirty days.

Note: Daily and weekly plans are a great way to make sure that you are maintaining your monthly priorities and staying focused. Free printable planners can also be found on our website: AdoreThemParenting.com/Book-Resources.

January
Monthly Intentions

1. What are some things that I can do to improve my own well-being?

_____

_____

_____

2. How can I support and connect with my partner?

_____

_____

_____

3. What do my kids need me to make a priority?

_____

_____

_____

4. What will I need to focus on for work?

_____

_____

_____

5. Which household tasks or projects need my attention?

_____

_____

_____

*

Focus on You: Take Time for Yourself

As parents, normal life seems to stop in November and December as the holidays become our main focus. We throw ourselves into parties with friends, school celebrations, volunteering, visiting family, shopping, cooking, cleaning, and plenty more. Each year, we try to create amazing memories throughout this season—and hopefully still manage to find time to pause and enjoy the magical chaos ourselves. It's a lot!

But now that it's January, we are trying to regroup and refocus. Starting a new year can feel both daunting and thrilling at the same time. There is a balance between trying to recover from the whirlwind of the end of last year, focusing on what's to come with renewed energy, and simply managing the reality of day-to-day life with our families and our careers.

Life keeps moving forward whether we feel prepared or not, so we may as well start the year with a fresh perspective! Instead of losing time and getting bogged down in mundane obligations, how can we approach our lives with a sense of adventure? What will this new year bring for us and our family? What will we be able to accomplish individually and together? And what will we be able to learn over the course of the next twelve months before the next New Year's Eve ball drops?

Adopting a sense of adventure doesn't mean that you need to become supermom or bat-dad. We simply want to help you create a strong, stable foundation for both you and your family. The strategies laid out in this book are meant to help you find balance and stability in your daily life as a parent. When daily life feels more manageable, you'll be in a better place to handle the more challenging moments as well. There are many small strategies that you can start implementing right now that will result in significant, positive changes over the month ahead. Take it one step at a time, one day at a time, and one month at a time to start this year off right!

Accept that You Are Amazing

New Year, New You. Right? That's the message that we seem to be hearing, and it can be inspirational. We just need to make sure that we take that message in a positive direction rather than a negative one.

3

Wanting to improve yourself this year does not mean that you weren't awesome last year. We are always learning and growing. We might look back on past decisions and cringe, but oftentimes we were doing the best that we could in that particular moment. So while we want to continue down a path of self-improvement this year, we need to first acknowledge how important we are to our families, our communities, and to our colleagues. Pause. Take a deep breath. And hear these words:

You are important. You are needed. You are loved.

One of the most incredible parts about being a parent is that our kids manage to love us despite our flaws. Little kids could teach a master class on wiping the slate clean and starting a new moment with a smile! It is okay for us to make mistakes alongside our children, and we get bonus points if we use those mistakes as teaching moments. We don't have to be perfect for our kids—just like they don't need to be perfect for us.

There is power in that imperfection! As parents, we are the glue that holds everyone together. We manage the schedules, keep track of all the items, calm the nightmares, make sure there's food in the house, give multiple "brush your teeth" reminders, and still manage to plan fun activities from time to time. And that is only within our own homes. We are also active members of our communities who volunteer at school, church, and other organizations. We may work inside or outside of the home, or we might work in a hybrid situation with a little of both. And we have friends, family members, and partners that we deeply care about.

We are important to so many people. And while that can feel heavy at times, it is a beautiful responsibility to carry. Look around and take notice how much you're valued within your tight-knit circle. These people love you, depend on you, and respect you even if they don't express it on a regular basis.

Make Your Moments Count

Since we have so many other people relying on us, it can be hard to take the time to focus on ourselves. It can even make us feel guilty. Because if we take time for ourselves as individuals, doesn't that mean less time for our loved ones? Not necessarily.

It's very common for us to get bogged down in our daily lives and resort to going through the motions. There were days as a stay-at-home mom to young children when I was physically there for my kids, but I wasn't really connecting with them. On those days when my kids and I were only coexisting in the same space together, I wasn't doing anything to fill up their emotional buckets; but I wasn't doing anything to reenergize myself either! We don't have to be having deep bonding moments with our kids every moment of every day—sometimes coexisting and meeting their needs is good enough. But on those days or in those moments, why not let the focus be on something that you need as a parent?

One of my favorite guilt-free hacks is covertly listening to podcasts. When my kids were little, I had a daily routine where we would all snuggle on the couch in the afternoon and turn on their favorite movie to watch for the hundredth time. I would bring my phone, pop in my earbuds, and hit play on a podcast. It was a way for me to enjoy a mom moment with non-cartoon entertainment, while they enjoyed a kid moment, while we all enjoyed a family moment. Instead of dreading watching the same boring movie over and over again, I looked forward to those calm afternoons together.

It is unreasonable to think that we should be spending every moment of every day focusing on others. It's an impossible task. I want to challenge you, as you start this new year, to think about how you are spending your time throughout a regular day. You are probably already stealing small moments for yourself, but instead of feeling guilty about those moments, own them! We shouldn't be sneaking around our own homes hiding from our children and our partners. It's normal and necessary to reenergize ourselves throughout each and every day. Self-care doesn't have to be extravagant. We just need to check in with ourselves every once in a while.

*

Connect with Your Kids: Set New Goals

As the holiday festivities come to an end, it can be tough for kids to get back into a normal routine; but it is our job as parents to help them with that transition. As we reflect on the past year and set intentions for the year ahead, it's a great time to teach our kids how to set goals and work toward them, with the aim of inspiring them to try new things and grow in different areas of their life.

Whether it's saving their allowance to buy something they want, studying to achieve a certain grade on a test, or practicing soccer drills in the backyard so that they can score in the upcoming game, we can help our kids set achievable goals, find motivation to work toward those goals, and figure out a plan to successfully accomplish them. We want our kids to take ownership of their own plans and work hard because they want something—not because we want it for them. It's important for kids to learn that it's okay to try, fail, and then try again. If we let our kids practice these goal planning steps now, they will be more prepared for the future. Motivation, work ethic, and goal planning will all be crucial when they are trying to keep up with college classes, secure a decent job, and eventually support families of their own.

Part of the goal planning process is teaching our children how to set realistic goals. Dreams are fabulous, and everyone should have them! But if you do not also incorporate realistic plans, you may find your children getting discouraged. Realistic goals can still be inspirational, but they have to remain attainable. Let's help our kids adopt a healthy balance when it comes to dreaming big and setting achievable goals.

Create a Wishing Wall
A Wishing Wall will captivate your kid's attention and introduce them to the concept of goal setting. All you need are some sticky notes, a few markers, a little guidance, and you can turn any wall, door, or closet into a Wishing Wall.

Discuss with your children what it means to set a new goal, and ask them a few questions to inspire their thinking. What new things would they like to try? How can they make a positive difference in someone else's life and their own life? Is there something that they would like to accomplish? Is there something that they would like to save for?

Now help them brainstorm what they will need to do in order to work toward their new goals. Explain that goals can range from small to big. Some can be achieved quickly, while others might take years of hard work and dedication. They can be general goals like "not getting so mad at your siblings" to more specific, like "reading a new and challenging chapter

6

book." Something easy and free like "holding doors for people with a smile" to something that requires saving money and planning such as "visiting a new city."

Once everyone has some good ideas, grab a pack of sticky notes and some markers. Pick a spot in the house for your Wishing Wall. Each child could have their own Wishing Wall on the back of their bedroom door, or you could put a family Wishing Wall right in the kitchen. Write down one goal on each sticky note, and then place it on the chosen spot. You can organize these goals in rows or place them randomly! If you choose to keep your Wishing Wall organized, think about categorizing goals from easy to hard, or from goals that are achievable quickly to goals that might take much longer.

Once you finish creating the Wishing Wall, check in with your kids often and ask them about their progress. Encourage them to keep working toward those goals! Once they accomplish a goal, they can add it to their journal or figure out some other special way to mark that accomplishment. The great thing about sticky notes is that they can easily be removed, replaced, reordered, and replicated again and again.

Goal Planning Worksheet

In addition to a Wishing Wall, try to bring in other activities this month that incorporate goal planning. This skill can be very helpful even for young kids as long as it is made accessible to them. One way to do this is to expand on goals you brainstormed for the Wishing Wall by having your kids fill

Goal Planning Questions

Have your kids work through these questions and make a plan for themselves! (Print copies of this worksheet by going to AdoreThemParenting.com/Book-Resources.)

- I am good at ....
- I need to work on ....
- My plan to improve is ....
- I will know my plan is working if ....
- If my plan doesn't work, then I will ....

out a simple goal planning worksheet. From an early age, kids can grasp the concepts outlined here. They may need your help brainstorming, writing things down, or following through on their plan; but . . . they are capable of thinking toward the future in this meaningful way!

Mail Delivery at Home

Mail Delivery is a fun activity for kids of all ages because you can make it as simple or as complicated as you'd like. The premise is to set up a mail system in your house and customize it according to what your kids would enjoy.

For older children, this system is a great way for them to be able to communicate with parents and siblings. Let them take control of the planning process and see what they come up with! Encourage them to write you a weekly letter telling you about their week and updating you on their goals. And then write them a letter back filled with compliments and little silly secrets for the two of you. Decorating their own mailbox is an afternoon craft project in and of itself, and then the letters and mail delivery are an ongoing special activity.

For preschoolers and kindergarteners, mailboxes are a great way to let them start working on their letters and name. Have them create a mailbox for each room of the house. You can write the name of each room on the mailboxes for them so they can start to recognize those words. And then they get to deliver mail around the house. They can write their own letters and make their own drawings for special deliveries.

For toddlers, simply cut a slot in the top of a shoe box and give them some pieces of paper to put in their mailbox. They will love putting the pieces in and taking them out over and over again. Toddlers also love decorating the box and papers with stickers and crayons. (Looking for more indoor kid activities? Jump to page 36!)

Taking even a few moments out of each day to talk with each other can make a meaningful difference in your family relationships. Make an effort to share little moments with them throughout each day and treat your kids like the awesome sidekicks that they are. Whatever activities you choose to try with your kids this month, keep in mind that the goal is to simply settle down from the holidays, reconnect as a family, and look forward to the year ahead together.

*

Work from Home: Find a Balance

Working from home is a great option that is growing in popularity for employees and employers. If there is one thing that recent events have shown us, it is that a lot can be accomplished at home. And thanks to modern technology, it can actually be achieved pretty easily. Businesses can continue to operate without the expensive overhead. Colleagues can communicate through video conferencing, and there are many resources that allow us to stay on top of it all while outside of a main office.

Previous generations did not have the options that we have today, and it can be a luxury to choose where you want to clock in each day—home, the back porch, a local coffee shop, a picnic table at the park, or maybe even the beach? Working remotely definitely has its perks, but it also has its challenges. Especially when you have young kids who constantly seem to need your attention. You may need to adjust your goals and expectations, but after ten years of working from home, I can confidently say that you can successfully work from home with the right tools and strategies.

Working from home is very different from working in a professional office space. The advantages are that you can get away with working in your pajamas. You have more control over your schedule. You can spend more time with your children, and even take a break to run around with them outside. You can start a load of laundry and enjoy a homemade lunch with your kids. You are also hopefully saving money on childcare, and you don't have to worry about a commute which can save a lot of time and, again, more money.

But while there are many perks, there are also unique challenges that you will face. Like multitasking work calls while getting your little one snacks. Helping a child in the bathroom, and then shifting to a professional tone when responding to emails. No longer will you be able to work for eight consecutive hours; instead it will have to be done in blocks of time. And you might find yourself missing the adult interactions and office small talk, as it has now been primarily replaced by conversations with your children or your neighbor.

Throughout this book, we'll be covering different strategies for effectively working from home; but first, we want to share a few important themes that will help you find your own balance.

Put the Kids First

This tends to be one of my parenting philosophies in general—for better and for worse. But let me explain . . . I have found that if I can meet my children's needs first, I can then get more accomplished. I've tried diving right into my work, thinking that maybe I can get a few things done before the kids need me. And instead, I am being constantly interrupted and repeatedly responding, "Give Mommy five more minutes." This scenario doesn't let me put out my best work, and all of us end up feeling frustrated!

My strategy to help alleviate these types of scenarios is to set the kids up first. I might need to run around outside for thirty minutes with them, or sit on the floor and play Barbies. I give them my undivided attention and listen closely to what they want to tell me throughout that time together. I also enjoy creating a unique play setup for my kids. Setting up a village for their current favorite characters always seems to be a hit. Some days we let my old Polly Pockets drive around in Matchbox cars, and other days we build a LEGO zoo for all of the animals. Add in a few snack bowls and water bottles, and I can tiptoe over to my computer for some uninterrupted work time. While I don't stick around for the actual playing, I still get to be involved in the brainstorming fun of it all, and my kids were able to enjoy some quality time with me before I needed to turn my attention elsewhere. Simply meeting their needs first then allows me to focus on my work while they play independently. (Flip to page 156 to find more tips for helping your kids play independently!)

Be Consistent and Flexible

Working from home requires you to be both consistent and flexible. You'll need to practice consistency because it's easy to get distracted or feel unmotivated when the dishes are piling up in the sink, or the kids are begging for a pool day. You will have to stay dedicated to make this situation work (and to keep collecting that paycheck). You can only hit that snooze button so many times before you need to get up and get focused.

You will also need to be flexible. And no, these two things aren't total opposites. You can remain consistent while also going with the flow. It's a necessary skill as a work-from-home parent, because no two days are the same when you have little ones running around. One day you might be super productive and get the majority of your work done in the morning while everyone plays in harmony. And the next day, you might feel more like a referee and won't be able to get to a single email before lunchtime.

This past year I was trying to work from home while also homeschooling my three children for the semester. This definitely presented some new challenges that we all had to adjust to. I quickly realized that I had to come up with a new routine that kept us all productive and organized. Every morning I would get up early, check my email, and make a list of my priorities for the day. I usually spent an hour responding to whatever was time sensitive, and I let the rest of my contacts know that they could expect to hear from me later in the day.

Once I had a handle on my workload for the day ahead, we would switch over to schoolwork. The kids and I would swap places, and they would jump onto my computer or their devices, and start their lessons. I would temporarily do what I could from my phone and notepad at the kitchen island, and float back and forth as my kids had questions or needed help.

A block of time spent on work, a block of time with the kids, and repeat. Eventually you will figure out what works best for you and your family. You'll have to balance flexibility and consistency as schedules and situations continually change, but the work-from-home strategies explained throughout this book will help spark new ideas and inspiration that you can apply to your own life.

*

Monthly Reflections

Since parenting requires so much from us day after day, it can be hard to slow down and take the time to reflect on what's working and what we need to change. You might be tempted to breeze past these monthly checkpoints, but we highly recommend that you take a few minutes to stop and reflect on the past month while it's still fresh in your mind.

There are a few reasons to do this exercise each month. First of all, it encourages you to live and parent more mindfully. It is a checkpoint so that you don't continue on the same path month after month, year after year. If something isn't working well for you and your family, you have the opportunity to identify that and begin to correct it!

It also gives you the opportunity to highlight and appreciate the things that *are* going well. Feeling gratitude for amazing people and moments in your life will lead to even more positivity in the following month. We want to train our brains to see the bright side, and monthly reflections are a simple way to do that.

Once you work through your monthly reflections, you may want to share your thoughts with trusted loved ones in your life. It is a great way to share insight with your partner, your coworkers, and your friends. You can share new ideas with them, and they will be able to support you moving forward as well!

January
Monthly Reflections

Five Highlights
What were your favorite moments from the month?

_____

_____

_____

Four Things You Focused on
What took up the most brain power this month?

_____

_____

_____

Three Game Changers
What were those a-ha moments?

_____

_____

_____

Two Things You Didn't Get to
Do you need to get to them next month?

_____

_____

_____

One Disappointment
Did you take time to grieve that moment?

_____

_____

_____

Next Month
What do you want to continue for the next month?

_____

_____

_____

What do you want to change for the next month?

_____

_____

_____

Notes

_____

_____

_____

_____

_____

_____

_____

_____

Chapter 2

February

Valentine's Day is at the top of everyone's mind this month. In this chapter, you will find positive tips and strategies to help you establish a stronger foundation with your partner, your kids, and your friends by focusing on shared priorities and great communication. We discuss ways to help your kids navigate their own friendships. And we give practical tips for communicating promptly and professionally despite the chaos of working from home.

*

Monthly Intentions

At the beginning of each month, we'll leave space for you to prioritize, plan, and prepare. As parents, our lives can start to feel like a series of small emergencies. One simple way to keep things organized is to set clear priorities and plan accordingly for the month ahead. Answering these five questions at the start of each month only takes a few minutes, but it will help you feel organized and ready to tackle the next thirty days.

Note: Daily and weekly plans are a great way to make sure that you are maintaining your monthly priorities and staying focused. Free printable planners can also be found on our website: AdoreThemParenting.com/Book-Resources.

February
Monthly Intentions

1. What are some things that I can do to improve my own well-being?

   _____

   _____

   _____

2. How can I support and connect with my partner?

   _____

   _____

   _____

3. What do my kids need me to make a priority?

   _____

   _____

   _____

4. What will I need to focus on for work?

   _____

   _____

   _____

5. Which household tasks or projects need my attention?

   _____

   _____

   _____

*

Focus on You: Create a Solid Foundation

The month of February centers around relationships but not just romantic ones. Leading up to Valentine's Day, we want to make our significant other feel special and help our kids navigate their own friendships; but strong relationships require work throughout the entire year. You may enjoy grand romantic gestures each February, but love is so much more than that. The beauty of everyday family life is that you are sharing your true self with the people around you. It is raw, personal, and requires a huge amount of trust to simply be yourself—at your best and at your worst.

Our partners and our kids know us better than anyone else, which can cause conflict from time to time; but it also helps us to grow together. When you are able to feel connected with your partner, you will be able to stay more tuned in to your family as a whole. When you maintain a balance of support from your own friendships, you will be better able to help your kids through their own emotional ups and downs.

February provides you with the opportunity to bring all of these relationships to the forefront, open the lines of communication, and figure out what is going to work best for you and your family. Every relationship looks different, and every season of life brings unique challenges. Partnerships and friendships naturally ebb and flow, and we need to adopt a sense of flexibility so that we can find strength in those changes rather than letting them hurt us.

Life with Your Partner

Do you remember when you first started dating your loved one? The excitement, butterflies, special date nights? You probably found their quirks endearing or even charming. But after a few years and a baby or two (or more), life can feel very different.

After more than a decade of marriage and multiple kids, life has changed for my husband and me. With each child our life has had to shift. Instead of traveling to exotic places, we explore anywhere a packed SUV can take us. Instead of going out to fancy dinners, we order takeout sushi and enjoy it on our patio. Instead of last-minute movie dates at the theater, we look forward to movie nights at home surrounded by our kids, dogs, popcorn, and Disney characters.

However, I wouldn't trade these changes in our life for the world! Our home is filled with love and laughter on a daily basis. There is a never-ending list of family adventures that we get to enjoy through our children's eyes. And watching my husband parent our children has only increased my love and appreciation for him.

I once read that a successful marriage is falling in love with the same person over and over again. And now after being with someone for nearly two decades, I completely agree! Life changes. People change. Our likes, dislikes, interests, and dreams change. Even the way that we show our love can change. So it makes sense that as we keep moving through life and going through new experiences, our relationships will change too.

Some phases will be easier than others. There will be times when you will feel in sync with one another, and times when you feel like you're navigating new territory with a stranger. It can be stressful, hard, and downright complicated. And you may start to panic when you lose the butterflies, grow apart, or find yourself feeling more frustrated than in love.

When this happens, someway and somehow you need to find that common ground again.

Those honeymoon butterflies haven't totally disappeared; they have been replaced with little human beings. And those feelings of infatuation have evolved. They grew into something much deeper, which is a lasting love based on true friendship and a solid partnership. Even when the romance fades, we can respect one another, appreciate the value that each person brings to the relationship, and share dreams for our family's future.

Appreciate the Small Things

Marriage can't always be about grand gestures and romantic getaways. It is more often about those quiet moments that go unnoticed. These small moments are the building blocks for something incredible, especially when children are in the picture. Take the time to notice how your house functions. What kind of rhythm have you and your partner found that works for the whole family? How often does something happen without even having to discuss it—you just divide and conquer?

Meals get made, kids get bathed, laundry gets switched to the dryer, groceries get put away, books get read, and items gradually get checked off the to-do lists. As we find our rhythm as a family, we tend to pass off responsibilities in a more fluid way. We start to understand the needs of our children as well as our own needs, and we gradually learn how to balance them all. We stop keeping score and start doing what needs to be done.

There is something profoundly beautiful about that type of relationship, because it isn't about a fancy date night or snuggling at sunset. It is simply about living together and being beside each other through both the exciting and the mundane.

Sometimes deep conversations need to be had. Sometimes we need to remind each other of our mutual ambitions and focus on the bigger picture. Sometimes we need to say "I'm sorry," and let the past be in the past. But the goal is always to come together, regroup, and begin working toward those shared priorities once again. It's certainly not always easy, and in particularly hard seasons, outside counsel or support may be required. But by honestly assessing where your relationship is today and committing to work through areas of tension, you can prevent issues from building over time.

My husband and I are building a life together. We are expanding our careers. We are raising our children and trying to create fun lasting memories along the way. We are deepening our relationship with one another and our family as a whole. And once we get through the hard stuff, there is always a happy outcome waiting for us on the other side. The challenges make us stronger. They give us an opportunity to readjust, shift our priorities, and try again. And we remind ourselves that this is a journey that we have committed to together.

At the end of the day we both want the same thing—what is best for our family. This means that we will each need to make sacrifices along the way. Compromises will need to happen. But in the end, we know we will all be in a much better place for it. Right now, during this phase in our life and parenting journey, our shared priority is our children. And as long as we keep them our primary focus, it will keep bringing us together again and again.

The One-Week Challenge

Once kids come along, life gets busy . . . really busy! A lot of the day is spent focusing on what needs to be done and figuring out who will do what. Unfortunately, in the midst of all of this, we (understandably) forget to do small things for our loved one. The following small gestures can make a big difference and help you both feel more connected and in-tune with each other. Commit to taking this one-week challenge and finding a simple way each day to show your partner what he or she means to you.

Small Gestures for Your Partner

Print copies of these ideas at AdoreThemParenting.com/Book-Resources.

Sunday: Pick a task that is usually your partner's responsibility and do it for them.

Monday: Make coffee (or another favorite drink) for your partner and have it ready for them in their favorite cup.

Tuesday: Text your partner three compliments at random times throughout the day.

Wednesday: Bring home a small gift to show that you've been thinking about them.

Thursday: Set aside time to dream about the future together.

Friday: Snuggle, hold hands, and enjoy a shared snack while you watch a movie together.

Saturday: Carve out an hour for just the two of you without your phones.

*

Connect with Your Kids: Help Your Kids with Friendships

Thankfully, many schools now require kids to give out Valentines to every child in the class, but there can still be challenging dynamics at play. Close groups of friends may gift special treats and find this time of year fun and exciting, while others might be feeling sad and left out. As parents, it is part of our job description to help our kids figure out this weird world of friendship. We want to help our kids choose good friends, while also being thoughtful friends themselves.

Kids may not automatically understand the unspoken rules of friendships. When my children have come home from school hurt and confused by an interaction, it has provided us with an opportunity to talk more about those issues. The goal is always to equip my kids with the tools that they need to establish great friendships and recognize the not-so-great ones. I don't want to make all of the decisions for them, because what will they do when I'm not there to guide them?

In my own life, I have seen the impacts of surrounding yourself with different types of people. While we like to think that we are our own person, we are heavily influenced by the world around us. Knowing this, I strive to surround myself with people that represent what I want to be and how I want to live my life. And I regularly remind my kids that we are able to choose who we spend the most time with, and why we need to make those decisions carefully.

Learning Moments

My daughter experienced this lesson firsthand with a group of friends in elementary school who were not being kind to other classmates. My daughter did not have any of this behavior directed toward her, and she did not engage in anything hurtful either. But, we both saw what was going on, and it offered the perfect opportunity to talk about the importance of picking friends.

We simply talked about how even though these other girls were fun to play with, they did not always make good choices. My daughter was able to understand that even though the hurtful words did not come from her own lips, those words left another friend hurt in her presence. Our little talk didn't last long because I only wanted to make her aware of how other kids might be feeling around her. The goal was not to make her feel shamed or overwhelmed, but merely to plant seeds for future growth.

A few weeks later, something interesting happened. My daughter had started recognizing this behavior more and more, and she made her own decision to focus on friendships with some other kids instead. She was still kind to those other classmates and played with them from time to time, but she did not seek out extra time with them. I never told her that she had to drop a friendship (because I truly believe in being nice to everyone), but I was able to encourage her to seek out good friends.

By listening and keeping the lines of communication open, we can help guide our children without pushing them away. Just like you are reading this book for new ideas and ways of looking at things, our kids are often very receptive to new information. We can make a difference in our kids' lives by offering a few extra moments of our time and patience.

What Makes a Good Friend?

The best way to make our message stick is to keep it simple and make it interactive! Kids especially love any opportunity for hands-on learning, and they are often drawn to visual lessons. Friendship can be a strange, abstract concept, but this activity makes a good friendship seem more tangible and concrete for kids.

Trace your child's hand onto a piece of paper. Or if you are feeling brave and don't mind getting a little messy, you can also paint your child's hand and then press it onto paper or a canvas. Once you have the handprint, write down the following five keys to being a good friend—one on each finger:

1. Be Kind
2. Be Fair
3. Be Truthful
4. Be Grateful
5. Be Trustworthy

As you do this craft, talk with your child about each key trait. What does being kind look like? What's an example of a time your child was truthful with a friend? And so on. Be sure to hang this craft somewhere that your child will see it regularly. It is a great reminder of both how to be a good friend and what to look for in others.

Friendship Challenge

The Friendship Challenge is another fun way to encourage your kids to show kindness to others. First, grab a small box, and let your kids decorate it with stickers and fun designs. Then talk about ways to be a good friend and things that we can do to make other people smile. It is so sweet to hear what our kids come up with for this task! If they need some help getting started, here are a few ideas:

- Hold the door for someone.
- Let someone else go first in a game.
- Give a friend a hug.
- Make a card for someone that is hurt or sick.
- Give someone (that is not a close friend) a compliment.
- Share your toys with someone.
- Sit with someone new at lunch.
- Play with someone who looks lonely at recess.
- Help a friend who might need you.
- Smile at everyone!

Write down each of these ideas on a slip of paper and place them in the box. Then each morning, have your kids pull out a slip of paper and get their Friendship Challenge for the day. They will come home with great stories of how they made someone smile, and they will probably have new ideas to add to the box as they go along! You can even have a nightly check-in around the dinner table where your kids update you on how their challenge went that day. It's a fun, interactive way to keep kindness as a priority in your family.

Friends Poster

What does it mean to be a good friend? To be honest, I still need this reminder as an adult! This easy craft project lets you and your kids highlight the most valuable aspects of friendship. You can make this poster as big or as small as you'd like. Poster board, canvas, construction paper, or even a simple piece of paper all work for this family craft. Older kids will love being creative and designing their own poster, while younger kids might need you to write the words for them and then they can decorate the rest. It also gives you a chance to practice letters with little ones. Write down the following and then decorate however you'd like!

FRIENDS
Forgive You
Respect You
Involve You
Encourage You
Need You
Deserve You
Support You

These lessons are great building blocks for helping our kids understand what it means to be a good friend and what to look for when choosing friends. They can also be a great reminder for us adults too! Relationships can get complicated. Friends pass in and out of our lives. But when we pause and reflect, we realize that these individuals have a lot of influence over our mindset and moods. So, while you are teaching your kids about friendships, make sure that you are also taking your own advice. Let the special people in your life know how truly appreciated they are. And if there are people who are not adding to your life in a positive way, you may need to reassess how much time you are spending with them. Genuine friends are worth more than gold—so find them and treasure them, and let the others be nice acquaintances that you say "Hi" to every now and then.

*

Work from Home: Communicate Professionally

We consistently hear about the importance of communication in our personal relationships, but how often are we considering the impact of our communication methods on our careers? Communicating within the workplace brings its own set of challenges since you are trying to balance coming across as professional, but also human. You want to be open and honest, without oversharing. And you want to be effective, without seeming manipulative. Even if you had settled into a good rhythm of interoffice communication at the workplace, working from home puts a different spin on things!

Shortly after we launched AdoreThemParenting.com, we began working with a large toy brand. We set up a fun video and photo shoot for the company with adorable babies playing with the company's toys. At some point during the day, the spokesperson from the company had the realization that Adore Them was simply a two-person operation. It was the two of us moms, running this company from our homes while juggling our own children. They expressed how impressed they were by the work that we had been doing and had assumed that we had an entire team working behind the scenes.

I don't share this to brag, but to explain that professional communication really matters. We handle ourselves professionally, take our work seriously, and thankfully that shines through! The following tips are examples of how we communicate effectively and professionally while working from home.

Take Charge of the Situation

If you act like you are in control, then people will feel more comfortable. While working from home, there will be plenty of days when you feel pulled in different directions. Everyone and everything seems to need your attention, and you feel like you are completely at the mercy of everyone else. Even if you can't fully regain control in that moment, you can communicate as if you have everything handled.

While working from home, you may quickly realize how few of the doors in your house actually lock, and how much your kids love being by your side. I have taken numerous important phone calls on the floor of my son's bedroom because it is one of the only doors in our house that locks. I have also taken phone calls with my kids sitting in my lap under the promise that they will sit quietly until I'm off the phone. But even when you try to prepare, there are likely to be interruptions. And when that inevitably happens, you can stay calm and collected.

Nothing is more unsettling to the person on the other end of the phone than you scolding your kids and showing your (understandable) frustration. If you need to address your kids, simply do the following: Say, "I'm sorry, can I please put you on hold for one moment?" Mute the phone. Speak with your kids quickly. Jump back on the phone and say, "Sorry about that. I'm back!"

Think of your little ones as persistent coworkers. When you're in an office environment, there are always interruptions. People are popping their head into your office with pressing questions or just to say "hello" throughout the day. It is normal to have to put people on hold, but it is unsettling to

25

hear you put on your mom-voice or dad-voice and tell your child that they have to put their pants back on.

Respond Quickly

It is very frustrating when a project is being held up because you are waiting for one small piece of the puzzle. Or when you aren't sure if your email was actually seen, or if it ended up in the spam folder. As humans, when we don't get a response, we start to invent our own version. Our minds begin to get carried away. *They must be busy. Or are they upset about something and not getting back to me? Maybe they're not busy or upset, they're just unprofessional. They don't even care about this project. Maybe they aren't the right person to be working with on this.*

If you know that you think those thoughts, then flip that situation. You do not want to be the person that others are wondering about. Don't leave communication up to the imagination!

Responding quickly makes you look courteous, professional, and trustworthy. And the quick response doesn't have to be the full response. You can simply reply to an email with something along the lines of, "Thank you for sending this over! I will take a look at it and get back to you." People simply want to know that you received their message and are taking it seriously. Sending them back two sentences is a quick way to establish trust and goodwill.

Since most of us carry smartphones around in our pockets, there is really no excuse for not responding promptly. It also allows us to keep our to-do lists a bit shorter because if a message comes in that you can quickly give an answer to, why wait until later? Get it off of your plate!

The exception to this rule is when you are purposefully taking time away from work. However, it is a great idea to give the people counting on you a heads-up before going off the grid (even for a few hours). You can set up auto-replies that let people know that you are not checking email currently, but will get back to them by a certain time or day. Simply keeping people in the loop is appreciated by all parties involved.

Don't Overshare

When I say to keep people in the loop, I mean to keep them updated professionally. You certainly don't have to share your entire reasoning for being away from your email. Early on in my freelance career, I did not understand the importance of this concept. Since I was a young mom working from home, I was worried that people expected me to be able to complete tasks instantly. In an attempt to show them that I was actually busy, I would make excuses that involved details of the mom side of my life.

Which one sounds more professional? "Sorry, I will have to get to this later. The baby is really fussy, and I'm trying to get him down for a nap." Or . . . "Thanks for sending this! I will work on it and get it back to you this evening." Employers, bosses, and coworkers don't need to know exactly why you can't do something at that particular moment. You are allowed to have your own life, but the people you work with are entitled to know when they can expect to receive your work. As soon as I started to shift my language in my communication, I began to feel more confident, and the people I was working for also felt more confident in my abilities. There were plenty of times when I responded to an email from my phone while breastfeeding a baby, but for all they knew, I was sitting in my home office typing it out on my computer.

Similarly, try not to overpromise. If there is already a deadline in place, then you should absolutely be striving to hit that deadline. But if there isn't already a deadline set, then don't create an arbitrary one for yourself. It might be tempting to say, "I'll get this to you by tomorrow." But why not just keep the language vague and give yourself a buffer by saying, "I'll work through this and let you know once it's ready." We are parents after all . . . you never know what the day might bring!

Shadow Their Language

Another simple way to establish great working relationships is to shadow the other person's language and communication style. Sales people for generations have been taught to mirror body language and repeat phrasing back to the person speaking. In the more digital age that we are working in, the same principles can still apply.

It is very easy to mirror the language that others are using in their communication when it comes to you via email, message, or text. Does the person use "Dear," "Hi," or "Hey" as their opener? Do they sign off with "Best," "Sincerely," or "Thanks?" Do they use certain terminology to explain things? Are they casual and using smiley faces, or is there a very formal feel to it? Once you get into the habit of noticing those details, you can simply shadow that communication style back to them. You are still sharing your own thoughts, opinions, and work in a way that is true to yourself; but you will likely benefit from packaging that message in the way that it will be best received.

There is so much time wasted in working environments because we are not being clear and efficient with our communication. While we can't control the behavior of everyone around us, we can at least make sure that we are communicating with purpose (and then hopefully others start to model the same thing). Whether you are sending an email or jumping on a phone call, keep in mind that the person on the other end is also swamped with various tasks. Try to keep things as short and simple as possible. Make an effort to organize your thoughts beforehand so that you can ask questions in an order that makes sense and take things one step at a time.

Working from home does not mean that all professionalism goes out the window. There are ways to adjust to this type of environment where interruptions and background noise come with the territory. And with professional communication, you are better able to advance in your career from your couch.

*

Monthly Reflections

Since parenting requires so much from us day after day, it can be hard to slow down and take the time to reflect on what's working and what we need to change. You might be tempted to breeze past these monthly checkpoints, but we highly recommend that you take a few minutes to stop and reflect on the past month while it's still fresh in your mind.

There are a few reasons to do this exercise each month. First of all, it encourages you to live and parent more mindfully. It is a checkpoint so that you don't continue on the same path month after month, year after year. If something isn't working well for you and your family, you have the opportunity to identify that and begin to correct it!

It also gives you the opportunity to highlight and appreciate the things that *are* going well. Feeling gratitude for amazing people and moments in your life will lead to even more positivity in the following month. We want to train our brains to see the bright side, and monthly reflections are a simple way to do that.

Once you work through your monthly reflections, you may want to share your thoughts with trusted loved ones in your life. It is a great way to share insight with your partner, your coworkers, and your friends. You can share new ideas with them, and they will be able to support you moving forward as well!

February
Monthly Reflections

Five Highlights
What were your favorite moments from the month?

_____

_____

_____

Four Things You Focused on
What took up the most brain power this month?

_____

_____

_____

Three Game Changers
What were those a-ha moments?

_____

_____

_____

Two Things You Didn't Get to
Do you need to get to them next month?

_____

_____

_____

One Disappointment
Did you take time to grieve that moment?

_____

_____

_____

Next Month
What do you want to continue for the next month?

_____

_____

_____

What do you want to change for the next month?

_____

_____

_____

Notes

_____

_____

_____

_____

_____

_____

_____

_____

_____

Chapter 3
March

This month can be difficult for families since there is often a lull in activities, the school year is dragging on, and the weather isn't ideal for outside fun. Here we lay out strategies for time management to help you feel less overwhelmed. We provide a variety of fun activities to keep the kids entertained and occupied until spring arrives. And we cover ideas for creating a workstation that allows you to be productive (even in a small space).

*

Monthly Intentions

At the beginning of each month, we'll leave space for you to prioritize, plan, and prepare. As parents, our lives can start to feel like a series of small emergencies. One simple way to keep things organized is to set clear priorities and plan accordingly for the month ahead. Answering these five questions at the start of each month only takes a few minutes, but it will help you feel organized and ready to tackle the next thirty days.

Note: Daily and weekly plans are a great way to make sure that you are maintaining your monthly priorities and staying focused. Free printable planners can also be found on our website: AdoreThemParenting.com/Book-Resources.

March
Monthly Intentions

1. What are some things that I can do to improve my own well-being?

_____

_____

_____

2. How can I support and connect with my partner?

_____

_____

_____

3. What do my kids need me to make a priority?

_____

_____

_____

4. What will I need to focus on for work?

_____

_____

_____

5. Which household tasks or projects need my attention?

_____

_____

_____

*

Focus on You: Manage Your Time

A few years ago, I had an important moment of realization. I was a stay-at-home mom, work-from-home mom, wife, friend, volunteer, sister, and aunt (among other things). I was trying to start a new business, and I was in the habit of saying "yes" to everyone around me. My focus was in too many places at once. Each day, I felt like I was trying to do (and be) so many different things; and yet, I couldn't do any of them to the best of my abilities. I would think about all of the areas where I felt like I was falling short, and I would get discouraged and downright mad at myself.

I was on a vicious hamster wheel of overcommitting and underperforming. I was home all day so of course the horrible question of, "What do you actually do all day?" was always weighing on me. The answer to that question was simple, yet complicated . . . "I spent all day doing something, but I feel like I got nothing done."

It is normal to daydream about our responsibilities fading away. Imagine what life would be like without sticky countertops to wipe, dishwashers to unload, laundry to be washed and folded, kids to dress, fights to break up, tangled hair to brush, or any other small task that takes time out of our days. Life as a parent feels like an ongoing version of *If You Give a Mouse a Cookie* where one task always leads to another task (and likely a new mess). But when I looked at my situation, I realized that there were really only three ways around it:

1. I could win the lottery and hire a staff of professionals.
2. I could give up the kids, pets, husband, and house.
3. I could learn to better plan my time.

Since I love my life and all of the craziness that comes with it and since I don't seem to have a lucky streak, I figured it was time to figure out a better way to manage my days.

Pick a Daily Focus

The strategy that I came up with has continued to work well for me for years now! It has also been so rewarding to see this same method work for fellow parents that have adopted it. It is a simple concept that you can start implementing today, and when you follow it consistently, it will gradually become a new, calmer way of life.

It is important to set priorities for each day. Some days my focus needs to be on my house, especially when there is a blanket of dog hair across my wood floors. Other days, I need to focus on my business. And most importantly, I need days to focus on my family. Of course, working from home means that every day will be a bit of a balancing act, but the way that I began structuring my priorities from day to day was different. I began planning my key focus for each day so that some days would be house days, some would be work days, and others would be family days.

House Days

I try to pick a day each week when we can stay home most of the day and get things done around the house. If the kids are home, then I am happy to have them help out! We go through the house cleaning room by room. The kids usually work to pick up everything and put it in its proper place, while I do more of the deep cleaning. The kids will take a small break after each room or two so that cleaning the whole house doesn't feel so overwhelming.

By knocking out the majority of our cleaning in one day, it allows us to enjoy the clean space for the rest of the week and only tidy up as needed. And when we are purposeful about picking up after ourselves, the house never gets too out of control. It is a great feeling when your home feels fresh and clean. And I have grown to enjoy these house days because they are a good, guilt-free, mindless break from other responsibilities.

Work Days

There are many days when my focus needs to be on my work, and I allow myself to dive deeper and spend more time at the computer on those days. Since I work from home, there will always be interruptions, and my kids will still need me throughout the day. However, on work days, I don't feel guilty about letting the kids watch extra TV, or explaining to them that they need to play on their own so that I can focus on the project at hand.

I am able to be extremely productive and stay focused on my work throughout these days because in the back of my mind I know that it is just my focus for today, and my kids (or my house) will get my undivided attention another day. I have heard from many work-from-home parents that struggle with the nagging idea that they should be switching loads of laundry between work emails. However, this multitasking interrupts your train of thought and makes it hard to stay motivated throughout the day. Instead, get as much done as you can on your work days so that you can go to bed that night feeling like you made real progress. (Visit AdoreThemParenting. com/Book-Resources for daily planner printables.)

Family Days

My favorite days are the family days! Sometimes we plan something special for a day trip, and other days we simply carve out the time to play games together and have a dance party. On family days, we don't worry about the dirty dishes in the sink, and we keep the focus on spending quality time together.

I once had a doctor tell me that it's not about the quantity of time you spend with your kids, it's about the quality of time you give them. I feel the importance of this sentiment because I am home all the time with my children, but if I don't organize and prioritize my days, I don't give them the meaningful, quality time that they crave. Your kids don't need your sole focus all of the time, but they do need it *some* of the time. Taking those days to tune in and truly listen to your kids will bring you closer together.

Instead of feeling like every single day needs to be balanced, try looking at the bigger picture. Are you finding a happy, healthy balance throughout each week? When we zoom out and give ourselves more than twenty-four hours to pack it all in, we can actually start to feel like we are accomplishing something!

*

Connect with Your Kids: Enjoy Easy Activity Ideas

By March, the novelty of the holiday gifts has worn off. There is downtime between sports seasons, and the kids are getting stir-crazy after having to spend more time indoors over the winter months. Even though you are exhausted yourself, you still need activity ideas to keep your energetic kids entertained. Over the years, we have gone down our fair share of Internet rabbit holes. We have tried the activities that require an hour of prep and clean up time, but only entertain your kids for a total of ten minutes. Instead, these simple activities are designed to keep your kids busy, engaged, and learning new skills.

Some of these strategies require a little extra effort on your part, and we know that can feel difficult when you are already overwhelmed. But we promise that the extra effort does pay off! Setting up a fun, engaging activity or spending some time connecting with your kids often leads to them being able to play happily without needing you for a while. And on those crazy days, keep breathing and remember that this is only a moment in time. Spring is right around the corner.

Stuffed Animal Hide-and-Seek
If you've ever tried to play hide-and-seek indoors, you know that the game gets old pretty quickly. There are only so many places that a person can hide in a house. And while a child might think it's fun to hide in the same spot over and over again, Mom and Dad deserve to have a little bit of fun too! So instead of hiding yourself, play hide-and-seek with a stuffed animal. Take turns hiding a stuffed animal (or any toy). You can get very creative with hiding spots for this game because stuffed animals can hide in cabinets, refrigerators, under the couch, or on the shelf in the closet. Since the hiding spots can be more difficult, you might need to give some "hot" and "cold" clues to help your kids. And once your kids get the hang of the game, encourage them to play it together with their siblings so that you can go get some other things done!

Mini Trampolines
Mini trampolines are a great way for kids to get out their excess energy when they aren't able to go play outside. The nice thing about these small trampolines is that they are safer than the full-size trampolines, they can be used in any room of the house, and can be stored away easily. Instead of buying a trampoline marketed to kids, look for the small, round exercise trampolines. They are typically more affordable, and since they're made for adults, they'll last much longer.

Tub Time
Think of your tub as a closed-in play area for your young kids and get creative! You'll be amazed how long kids will stay in the bathtub when

37

you aren't rushing to get them out and onto the next thing. The tub is the perfect place to let them paint or do other messy activities. Go to the dollar store and stock up on a bin of tub activities like watercolor paints and shaving cream that are fun to paint on the shower walls. Move the plastic building blocks into the bathtub for some building fun, and look through the playroom for animal toys, balls, cars, and other toys that can withstand the water.

My bonus tip for tub time is to make sure that you get to enjoy it too! Even though you have to be in the bathroom supervising the kids, you can still make that time productive. You can take your laptop into the bathroom and get some work done, deep clean the bathroom, or call a friend to catch up while you watch the kids playing happily. Think outside the box and make the most of it!

Balloons

Even though my kids are elementary school age now, I still keep a supply of balloons in the house. They love them! And they continually find creative uses for them. They play "keep the balloon in the air" and variations of balloon volleyball. And they enjoy doing mini experiments with the balloons like putting them in front of fans, playing with them in water, or testing out static cling.

If you want to get fancy, you can purchase different types of balloons. Get the long balloons and look up balloon animal tutorials (some of them are surprisingly easy), or buy rocket balloons that buzz around the room making silly noises and can be inflated over and over again.

Play Charades

The game of charades was invented in the early eighteenth century, and there's a reason that it's been around for this long—it's easy and it's fun! Kids of all ages can enjoy playing together, and you can get as creative as you want with the prompts. As you probably know, the idea of the game is to get others to guess what you're acting out without using words. You can purchase packs of charade cards that give you prompts of varying difficulty levels. These are sometimes helpful to have clear objects or concepts to act out. You can also simply search on the Internet for "charade ideas for kids," and pick from endless suggestions for your family.

However, my kids love coming up with their own charade ideas. They like to pick a theme of the night like "superheroes" or whatever else they happen to be into at the moment. It's a great way for kids to use their imagination, and for parents to be a part of the fun.

Painter's Tape

Painter's tape is an easy way to let your kids get creative and build mini worlds. Help your kids create racetracks, mazes, parking lots, hopscotch, rivers, castles, or anything else they can imagine. And then simply peel it up and throw it away. Your kids can stick it on the walls and the floors without having to worry about a huge mess or lasting damage (just don't leave it on for too long).

If your kids need some help getting started, this is a fun one for parents to help out with. Start building a painter's tape world for them, and then see where it goes! Grab some building blocks, some toy cars, a few barbies, and before you know it, you have a whole town.

Play Tents

Over the years, we have gathered a pretty large collection of kid pop-up tents. They spend most days in the closet, but every once in a while, we get them all out and set up a large maze for the kids to play in. You can put their favorite stuffed animals, dolls, or action figures in the tents with them. You can turn a tent into a ball pit. You can put balloons in the tents. Or, depending on the weather, you can take the tents outside for a literal change in scenery! They are lightweight and easy to set up and put away; and they allow you to create a new play area for your kids without actually having to leave the house.

The goal with all of these activities is to set up play stations that will inspire your kids to have fun on their own. You don't always have to leave the house to keep the kids entertained! And seeing those little faces light up is worth the time, attention, and effort.

*

Work from Home: Set up Your Workstation

In an office your employer typically has your workstation set up. However, when you work from home, this becomes your responsibility. Your employer might pay for your computer and printer, or give you an allowance for office expenses, but setting everything up will most likely fall on your shoulders.

I have had the pleasure of living in a very large home with an expansive home office space, and I have lived in a small apartment where my work area was in a tiny corner in the family room. I have also lived in several houses in between where each offered a different space for me to work. The one thing that I have learned from all of this is that if you have space, you will fit it; and your kids will find you no matter where you are.

The larger your office, the more papers you can hang on to. There are always fun furniture pieces and decorations that you can purchase. And who doesn't love shopping for office accessories? But is all of this extra stuff actually needed? Usually not. In fact, these larger spaces can become cluttered and lose their creative appeal over time. Even the famous Stephen King has said that he prefers a smaller room with a desk by a window to write his masterpieces. It offers fewer distractions and is much easier to maintain so that you stay focused on your actual work.

Designate Space

First you need a space. Whether this is a designated desk or one end of the kitchen table, you need a space that you will be able to work at consistently. While some people love to work in different areas of their home, or at the local coffee shop, it can still be helpful to have a home workstation that allows for a home base for productivity.

Try to think outside the box when you are considering different options for a home workstation. Do you have a formal dining room that you rarely use that would make a great home office? Would your desk fit in the corner of your bedroom and give you the option for more peace and quiet while working? Can you take over the kitchen counter that is usually covered with random papers anyway? Even an unfinished basement can work in a pinch with the help of a rug and some bright lamps.

The goal is to look around your home and think about how your family uses the space. If you have toddlers running around, you'll need to set

40

up a workstation that allows them to play happily while you keep an eye on them. If you have older kids, you may be craving a space where you can close the door and trust that everyone will be okay for a little while. These needs will shift and then so can your work setup.

Keep Things Close

When setting up your workstation, think through the items that you actually need in order to be productive. Try to keep this list of items as short and simplified as possible, and then keep those key things close by! When everything is at your fingertips, you'll be more productive, less distracted, and won't waste time looking for things that you need every day.

You might really only need your computer for most of your work tasks, but what else is helpful to you? I always like to have a notebook, pen, highlighter, and a planner. While I use my phone calendar for all of my appointments and our family's schedule, I like having a physical calendar that is solely work-focused. It helps to have something that I can write on, color code any special projects that I am working on, and make notes as I schedule out my work goals for the weeks ahead. I also like to keep a pair of headphones handy in case I need a little music pick-me-up or need to drown out some background noise for more focused tasks. For me and my line of work, these are my necessities, and the rest is all just a bonus. If needed, I could pack all of this into my computer bag and set up anywhere I desire.

If you live in a small space, you could have a drawer dedicated to these necessities in any room of the house so that you could get out your work and put it away quickly as you clock in and clock out. If you want to splurge a little, you could also purchase one of those tiered carts to roll around from room to room depending on where you want to work for the day.

You really don't need anything fancy to make working from home a success! You can set up a productive workstation anywhere and at any time. Think about the flow of your home and the needs of your kids. Keep the necessities to a minimum. Stay organized and regularly declutter. And don't hesitate to change things up whenever you need some new inspiration.

*

Monthly Reflections

Since parenting requires so much from us day after day, it can be hard to slow down and take the time to reflect on what's working and what we need to change. You might be tempted to breeze past these monthly checkpoints, but we highly recommend that you take a few minutes to stop and reflect on the past month while it's still fresh in your mind.

There are a few reasons to do this exercise each month. First of all, it encourages you to live and parent more mindfully. It is a checkpoint so that you don't continue on the same path month after month, year after year. If something isn't working well for you and your family, you have the opportunity to identify that and begin to correct it!

It also gives you the opportunity to highlight and appreciate the things that *are* going well. Feeling gratitude for amazing people and moments in your life will lead to even more positivity in the following month. We want to train our brains to see the bright side, and monthly reflections are a simple way to do that.

Once you work through your monthly reflections, you may want to share your thoughts with trusted loved ones in your life. It is a great way to share insight with your partner, your coworkers, and your friends. You can share new ideas with them, and they will be able to support you moving forward as well!

March
Monthly Reflections

Five Highlights
What were your favorite moments from the month?

_____

_____

_____

Four Things You Focused on
What took up the most brain power this month?

_____

_____

_____

Three Game Changers
What were those a-ha moments?

_____

_____

_____

Two Things You Didn't Get to
Do you need to get to them next month?

_____

_____

_____

One Disappointment
Did you take time to grieve that moment?

_____

_____

_____

Next Month
What do you want to continue for the next month?

_____

_____

_____

What do you want to change for the next month?

_____

_____

_____

Notes

_____

_____

_____

_____

_____

_____

_____

_____

_____

Chapter 4
April

There tends to be a renewed energy in the air throughout this month, and we want to put that positive outlook to good use. This chapter covers concrete ways to improve your self-confidence so that you can feel more fulfilled and secure in who you are. We provide step-by-step parenting advice for setting healthy expectations for your kids. And while you're in spring cleaning mode, we share home organization strategies that foster independence in your children to help reduce the interruptions throughout your work day.

*

Monthly Intentions

At the beginning of each month, we'll leave space for you to prioritize, plan, and prepare. As parents, our lives can start to feel like a series of small emergencies. One simple way to keep things organized is to set clear priorities and plan accordingly for the month ahead. Answering these five questions at the start of each month only takes a few minutes, but it will help you feel organized and ready to tackle the next thirty days.

Note: Daily and weekly plans are a great way to make sure that you are maintaining your monthly priorities and staying focused. Free printable planners can also be found on our website: AdoreThemParenting.com/Book-Resources.

April
Monthly Intentions

1. What are some things that I can do to improve my own well-being?

   _____

   _____

   _____

2. How can I support and connect with my partner?

   _____

   _____

   _____

3. What do my kids need me to make a priority?

   _____

   _____

   _____

4. What will I need to focus on for work?

   _____

   _____

   _____

5. Which household tasks or projects need my attention?

   _____

   _____

   _____

*

Focus on You: Improve Your Confidence

Becoming a parent can feel like it changes you on a fundamental level. We are wired to lose ourselves in our children, and it can be a beautiful transformation. Once we become a parent, we learn new things about ourselves and dig deeper into our strengths than ever before. But the huge responsibility of raising our children also brings up a lot of self-doubt.

We care so much about our children that we start to second-guess every decision that we make. We read conflicting advice, we overanalyze every situation, and we end up convincing ourselves that we are doing it all wrong. I am here to tell you that you are *not* doing it all wrong. The fact that you are reading this book is proof that you are trying to better yourself, which is all we can really do. We can try our best at any given moment, and we can stay open to the possibility of change.

Every child needs something different from us. While one child may love to roughhouse and be loud and boisterous, another may need you to sit quietly with them and follow their lead. There is no perfect way to parent. And just like with anything else, we will have good days and bad days. But once we accept the imperfection, we can stop looking for proof that we are doing it "right."

Building confidence within yourself is key to living a more fulfilling life. When you are feeling confident, you will be better able to enjoy everything and everyone around you. It opens you up to new opportunities, and it gives you a sense of freedom to make decisions that will be best for you and your family—regardless of what anyone else is doing.

Practice Following Your Instincts

We all need to practice following our instincts. Especially those of us who have spent a lifetime burying our gut feelings. Practice listening to your kids' cues. Practice going with your gut. Don't force yourself into a parenting style that makes you miserable. Keep listening to yourself, which can be harder than you think.

Part of following your instincts is not opening yourself up to other people's opinions. When we are feeling unsure of ourselves, we tend to ask around for opinions in hopes that it will make us feel better about our decisions. However, this strategy usually backfires, and it ends up making us feel even more insecure.

If the well-meaning stranger at the park asks how your baby is sleeping, you can lie and tell them that it's going well (even if your baby is up twenty times a night). Because chances are, the stranger will not be giving you life-altering advice. They will tell you the strategy that is working for their child, and you will walk away feeling like you are doing it all wrong. You may even feel like you should try the stranger's methods and go against your own instincts. Instead of putting yourself through all of that . . . smile, nod, make small talk, and then do what you know is best for *your* family.

Find a Few Good Friends

Friends with kids are the best. These trusted friends will eventually turn into your sounding board. They will help you remember that you are not alone in your struggles during any particular season of parenting. And they will allow you to process your own thoughts in a helpful way. Not everyone will want to discuss the ins and outs of potty training, but your friends that also have toddlers will. They will also listen to you and offer you advice without judgment because they are in exactly the same place that you are.

I understand that this is easier said than done, but it is possible to find those mom and dad friends. You will have to put yourself out there. You will have to leave the house (even when it takes an hour to get out the door). And you will have to put aside your own insecurities to make those connections . . . but it is so worth it! Join a local parent group, head to the park, join your library's storytimes. We are all looking for someone to connect with—especially when our kids are young. Find a few parents that you really click with and that have kids similar in age to your own.

Try Your Best

We all have good parenting moments and bad ones. But those bad moments often come when we can't muster up the energy or patience for anything else. A bad moment doesn't automatically make you a bad parent. Try your best, try to learn, try again, try to change. As long as you are trying to get better, you are on the right path. Change the things that don't work for you, and cling to the things that do!

It is also helpful to keep in mind that perfect parenting does not necessarily result in a perfect child, and the opposite is true as well. How many amazing people do we know that had difficult childhoods? Maybe we don't need to stress quite as much about every tiny parenting decision. Part of who our children will become is already etched into their DNA. I, of course, believe that parenting plays a huge role in raising children (otherwise why write this book?), but there is something reassuring in knowing that our child's destiny is not 100 percent in our hands.

It always amazes me to see how different siblings can be. You can think that you have this whole parenting gig figured out, just in time for the next child to have an entirely different personality from the minute they leave the womb. You have to adjust and be humbled by the fact that there is simply so much out of your control. Parenting is entirely about trying our best with the situation that we're handed at any given moment.

Act Confident

Yes, I'm telling you to fake it 'til you make it. We can't always *feel* confident, but we can always *act* confident. Think of a confident person. What does their body language look like? How do they talk? What do they do? You can emulate the appearance of a confident person as you continue to work on building your own confidence internally. And when you appear confident, people naturally begin treating you with more respect, which, in turn, boosts your confidence!

It is also important to work on being confident as a person, not only as a parent. Parenthood consumes us, which is part of what makes it so incredible. But if you were struggling with confidence before . . . this parenting thing will throw you for a loop! Take the time to think through your strengths, weaknesses, likes, and dislikes as a human being—then see how those things transition to parenthood. We have a terrible tendency to compare our own weaknesses to other people's strengths when all we really need to do is stay focused on our own journey. What do you enjoy about yourself, and how can you utilize your natural strengths in your personal life, as a parent, and in your career? Stay focused on what makes you amazing and be sure to showcase that to the world.

*

Connect with Your Kids: Set Healthy Expectations

Leaving the house with young kids can be downright stressful because going out in public can feel like a gamble. Are the kids going to throw a tantrum? Are they going to run around with boundless energy? Are they going to be disrespectful to the people that we interact with? Instead of worrying about what the day will bring, there are steps that you can take to make leaving the house both safe and manageable.

Being a mama with young children, I need order in my life to make it through the day. And what I have found to be most helpful is setting expectations—for both myself and my kids. Having healthy expectations creates order, gives guidance, and provides realistic requirements that everyone can live up to. Without these guidelines, chaos quickly takes over!

So what does this look like on a day-to-day basis? When we arrive at a destination, I talk to my kids before we get out of the car. This way they are able to focus on what we're talking about *before* becoming distracted by the fun, new environment. We talk about the expectations for that particular place, and the natural consequences of not meeting those expectations. If we go to a friend's house and aren't respectful of their home and toys, then we might not get invited back. There are so many built-in natural consequences for our actions, that we simply need to explain the realities of the situation to our children. This saves us from having to create new consequences for each scenario.

The benefit of taking the time to talk with your children about these expectations is that they begin to learn these things on their own. Since the goal is to raise children that make good choices even when Mom or Dad isn't there, we have to take the time to explain the reasoning behind our parenting standards. Each place that we go has slightly different rules, but we are able to talk about what is and is not acceptable in each of those different settings.

Print out these examples at AdoreThemParenting.com/Book-Resources and keep them in your car as helpful reminders.

When we're at the store, please . . .
- Hold my hand in the parking lot.
- Ask me before taking anything off of the shelf.

- Stay right beside me (or in the shopping cart).
- Walk through the aisles.
- Wait patiently in line and do not beg for candy at checkout.
- Be my helper, because I love shopping with you!

While you're at school, please . . .
- Listen to your teachers.
- Be kind to all of your friends and classmates.
- Give someone new a compliment.
- Look for someone lonely at lunch or recess and be a friend to them.
- Learn something new, and then tell me when you get home so we can learn together!

At the playdate, please . . .
- Take off your shoes when we go inside.
- Remember to say, "Please" and "Thank You."
- Share toys and ask to use toys before getting them out.
- Stay in the rooms they are entertaining in (do not go upstairs or downstairs without asking first).
- Be respectful of their property (do not jump on their furniture or run around inside).
- Have fun!

While we're at the playground, please . . .
- Hold my hand in the parking lot.
- Stay close to me so that I can always see and help you.
- Take turns with other kids and your siblings.
- Stay close to your siblings and/or friends (and help them if they need it).
- Watch where you are running so you don't bump into others.
- Have fun!

These expectation examples are all very basic and easy for a child to follow. And as your children grow older, these requests can be adjusted according to their age and your expectations. But the goal is always to keep these requests simple and easy to follow. Sure, you will have bad days here or there, but if your child is struggling to follow these expectations consistently then something else needs to change.

It's important to make sure that your expectations are reasonable for your child's age and ability. For example, it doesn't matter how many reminders you give a toddler, they will not be able to skip nap time and keep it together for an entire afternoon of shopping. It's also important to recognize when your child may need a little more support and guidance. They might need help developing coping skills that will help them handle interactions with other children on the playground.

There is also something to be said for not putting yourself in needlessly stressful situations. Having an outing end in arguments and tears is not good for anyone! Sometimes it might be better to leave your little one at home with a caregiver while you run to the store by yourself. I had a friend who always did her grocery shopping after 10:00 p.m. When I asked her about it, she cheerfully told me that it was easier for her to do it late at night without the kids than to take them all during the day. She said that she actually looked forward to her quiet, nighttime grocery routine. I loved seeing that she knew her limits and was willing to think outside the box!

We can't expect our kids to behave perfectly, 100 percent of the time. Even as adults, we don't do that! But giving these reminders before we hop out of the car does really help improve behavior. It is a fresh reminder that our actions have consequences, and that if we want to do the fun things in life, we have to challenge ourselves to be better—even when it's hard. We are able to work on these life lessons together as a family one trip at a time. And by taking it day by day, we are able to look back and honestly say that we have all improved in some way!

*

Work from Home: Make Your House Kid-Friendly

When I was pregnant with my third child, I gave this topic a lot of thought. How do I make my house more kid-friendly to encourage independence and safety? I knew that once the baby arrived, I would likely be in the middle of feedings or diaper changes when my then four- and two-year-old would be begging for snacks, drinks, or some form of entertainment. My goal became to meet as many of their needs as possible before the baby arrived. I went through all of the rooms in our house and made sure each one was safe and ready for my independent toddlers.

I knew that my kids would love the freedom, and I knew that I would love having fewer interruptions. However, safety was one of my main concerns. I had to figure out how to rearrange our house so that they could safely play, get their own snacks, and clean up after themselves. Since little kids are incredible at getting into things when you turn your back for even a second, I never let them out of my sight.

I set up baby gates to keep my toddlers from roaming upstairs while I sat on the couch feeding the baby. And I tried to think through each room in our house. I locked up and hid away anything fragile or messy, while making the fun and safe things more accessible to my kids.

Bathroom

In the bathrooms, I made sure that any unlocked cabinets contained things like towels, and not medicines or fancy soap bottles. I put step stools by each sink and toilet, and I filled the bath toy bucket with some new entertaining options. Look through the playroom for water-safe toys and add them to the bath time rotation to hold your child's attention!

While the kids played in the tub, the baby would often be happy in the sleeper, which let me sit in the bathroom and check my emails. The bathroom fan would often put the baby to sleep, and the older two enjoyed splashing in the contained space. It was great! I always made sure I had everything I needed at my fingertips for the next hour so that I never had to leave the room—not even for a minute.

Bedrooms

In each bedroom I had a few baskets of fun, busy toys. Kid bedrooms are a great place for doll houses, toy car garages, and other fun play setups; and you can put a nice basket filled with stuffed animals in your own master bedroom. I loved arranging things this way because then whichever room we ended up in for a feeding, some laundry folding, or even for a change of scenery, there was always something to keep the kids' attention so that they weren't trying to escape and find something else.

Kitchen

My biggest transformation was in the kitchen. I moved all of their snacks to the bottom of the pantry, and I put a stack of paper bowls on the bottom shelf. I then put a sleeve of small paper cups near a water cooler in our kitchen (that we already happened to have). You can also purchase multi-colored plastic cups, assign each of your kids a different color, and put a step stool in front of the kitchen sink.

My new rule was that the four-year-old could fill a snack bowl, and a cup of water, for her and her brother. But only if she asked me first, and if I was in a nearby room where I could still see them. I have always been very strict about the kids only ever eating in front of me. I have heard too many stories of children choking, and I think my paranoia has slightly scared my children into always following this rule. So, with that said, if your child is one to sneak snacks—these kitchen tips probably are not for you until your child is a bit older.

Because I was allowing my child a new responsibility that she was excited about, she was automatically eager to follow the rules. To our amazement, she rose to the occasion and loved helping her younger brother while I tended to the baby. And the two-year-old loved having his big sister doting on him. They relied on each other, and helped each other out. It was adorable to watch their bond grow through these small, simple tasks.

I have learned that watching my children grow and take on more responsibility can be fun and exciting—for both me and my kids! Once we create a safer, more controlled setting, we can let our kids safely explore their independence. They might surprise you with how much they can accomplish on their own when given the opportunity.

For me it took having another baby to rearrange my house. However, working from home is another great catalyst for making your home more kid-friendly! Walk through your house and make note of all of the areas where you have to tell your child "No." Then see if you can troubleshoot those areas to create a more peaceful environment. Think about how much more work you'll be able to get done if you are not constantly keeping your children out of harm's way.

This concept continues to be helpful even as your children get older. There are always things that we can do to help teach our children how to be more reliable, helpful, and self-sufficient. You can start early with age-appropriate tasks to avoid your child being the kid that doesn't know how to do their own laundry once they head off to college.

*

Monthly Reflections

Since parenting requires so much from us day after day, it can be hard to slow down and take the time to reflect on what's working and what we need to change. You might be tempted to breeze past these monthly checkpoints, but we highly recommend that you take a few minutes to stop and reflect on the past month while it's still fresh in your mind.

There are a few reasons to do this exercise each month. First of all, it encourages you to live and parent more mindfully. It is a checkpoint so that you don't continue on the same path month after month, year after year. If something isn't working well for you and your family, you have the opportunity to identify that and begin to correct it!

It also gives you the opportunity to highlight and appreciate the things that *are* going well. Feeling gratitude for amazing people and moments in your life will lead to even more positivity in the following month. We want to train our brains to see the bright side, and monthly reflections are a simple way to do that.

Once you work through your monthly reflections, you may want to share your thoughts with trusted loved ones in your life. It is a great way to share insight with your partner, your coworkers, and your friends. You can share new ideas with them, and they will be able to support you moving forward as well!

April
Monthly Reflections

Five Highlights
What were your favorite moments from the month?

_____

_____

_____

Four Things You Focused on
What took up the most brain power this month?

_____

_____

_____

Three Game Changers
What were those a-ha moments?

_____

_____

_____

Two Things You Didn't Get to
Do you need to get to them next month?

_____

_____

_____

One Disappointment
Did you take time to grieve that moment?

_____

_____

_____

Next Month
What do you want to continue for the next month?

_____

_____

_____

What do you want to change for the next month?

_____

_____

_____

Notes

_____

_____

_____

_____

_____

_____

_____

_____

Chapter 5
May

May brings Mother's Day and preparations for the kickoff of the summer season. This chapter encourages you to practice self-care with ideas that even the busiest parents can make time for. We share important advice and insight into how you can safely enjoy the swimming season ahead. And we cover practical tips for remaining productive despite interruptions and a new summer routine.

*

Monthly Intentions

At the beginning of each month, we'll leave space for you to prioritize, plan, and prepare. As parents, our lives can start to feel like a series of small emergencies. One simple way to keep things organized is to set clear priorities and plan accordingly for the month ahead. Answering these five questions at the start of each month only takes a few minutes, but it will help you feel organized and ready to tackle the next thirty days.

Note: Daily and weekly plans are a great way to make sure that you are maintaining your monthly priorities and staying focused. Free printable planners can also be found on our website: AdoreThemParenting.com/Book-Resources.

May
Monthly Intentions

1. What are some things that I can do to improve my own well-being?

_____

_____

_____

2. How can I support and connect with my partner?

_____

_____

_____

3. What do my kids need me to make a priority?

_____

_____

_____

4. What will I need to focus on for work?

_____

_____

_____

5. Which household tasks or projects need my attention?

_____

_____

_____

*

Focus on You: Practice Simple Self-Care

Since we get to celebrate Mother's Day this month, it feels relevant to highlight simple ways to care for yourself at different times throughout each day. Morning, noon, and night—parenting is a 24-7 job. We can get into the habit of meeting everyone else's needs all day long, only to collapse into bed feeling overwhelmed and unfulfilled. If we are not taking care of ourselves, it will start to take a negative toll.

After some simple a-ha moments, I realized that I could do little things for myself throughout each day. These things didn't take a lot of time or money, but they did start to make a difference in my life. I found myself becoming happier and a much better parent. By meeting my own needs on a daily basis, I have been able to give back so much more to my family, my relationship, my friendships, and even my work. And that's an amazing feeling!

Whether you use the following suggestions, or use some ideas of your own, the most important thing is that you remain consistent with these activities. Enjoying and appreciating a few small moments throughout each day will be helpful in the long run.

MORNING SELF-CARE IDEAS
Start Slow
Try to carve out a few minutes of calm alone time before diving into the rest of your day. If you are a morning person, you can set your alarm a little bit earlier and enjoy quiet time before the rest of your household wakes up. If you are not a morning person (like me), you can find a different way of sneaking in that peaceful time. I typically do not wake up until the first kid needs to be up and getting ready for school. However, after all of the morning drop-offs and craziness, I resist the temptation to dive right into my to-do list. I give myself a few quiet moments each morning to sip something warm and regroup before the rest of my day. It helps me to focus and mentally prepare for what lies ahead.

Gain Clarity
Mornings are also a great time to take a few minutes to meditate or pray. Doing this allows you to release your worries and stress, while gaining some

new clarity. Whether or not you prefer something spiritual, the goal is to focus on the positivity in your life and feel that appreciation before moving on with the rest of your day. You can find many uplifting books, calendars, apps, and newsletters that offer daily encouraging messages. By reading uplifting content early in the morning, it will help to shift your mindset as you go about the rest of your day!

Nourish Yourself

Treating yourself to one of your favorite breakfasts is an amazing way to embrace an early start. However, most of us parents have to make it through a mini-marathon each morning as we wake, dress, and feed our less than enthusiastic children. The last thing I feel like doing at 6:00 a.m. is whipping up some baked goods from scratch. Instead, I make a batch of mini muffins every Sunday, and I warm up a few each morning (with melted butter). It's delicious, and it's something that I am able to look forward to instead of scrambling to find something to eat. Whether you prepare a weekly quiche, jars of smoothies ready for the blender, or your own personal favorite make-ahead breakfast, consider how you can plan ahead to make your mornings easier.

AFTERNOON SELF-CARE IDEAS
Read Something for You

I find myself reading work emails, school newsletters, reviewing homework assignments, catching up on the news, and of course scrolling through social media. But it feels harder to find the time to actually sit down and read a book just for fun. I used to get frustrated that I didn't have uninterrupted time to get lost in a book anymore. There were always interruptions from cute little faces, and I started to give up on the idea of reading for pleasure at all. However, as with most things, a simple shift in perspective helped renew my love of reading and helped me to accept the phase of life that I am currently in.

As parents, we don't have to give up reading entirely, but we do need to change our expectations. Find books (like this one) where you can read a few pages at a time throughout the day or week. Think about reading like watching a TV series. You get little bits of the story as you go along, and eventually it all comes together in the end. I always keep a book in my car, which means that I usually find time in my day to read something that I enjoy. I appreciate the mental escape while sitting in the carpool line, speech therapy waiting room, or in the corner of the dentist office. Reading a few pages of a good book is much more refreshing and inspirational than subjecting myself to the land mines of social media.

Take a Bubble Bath

I know, I know, everyone tells you to take a bubble bath . . . but when is the last time you actually did? It might surprise you to learn that I aim for at least one per week! This might only be possible on the weekends or at night, but working from home might let you enjoy this relaxation idea in the middle of the day. It sounds indulgent, but if you needed to take a shower anyway, why not spend that time pampering yourself a bit more? Remind yourself that you are only doing this for twenty to thirty minutes, and then you'll jump back into the rest of your responsibilities.

Personally, I make the most of my bubble baths by adding Epsom salt, apple cider vinegar, and applying a face mask, and then twenty minutes later I walk out of that bathroom feeling like a new person! The key is to do what works for you. If you love candles, light some candles. If you want to listen to music, make a soothing playlist. Put together a basket that you keep in the bathroom with all of your favorite bath supplies so that you don't have to waste time collecting things from around the house. It should be quick, easy, and effective!

Play and Cuddle

Play with a pet or cuddle something soft. There is something about animals that can instantly calm us down. If you don't have pets at home, the next best thing is to cuddle up in a soft or weighted blanket for a few minutes. You can enjoy this almost anywhere in your house or even out on your porch. Connecting to ourselves through our sense of physical touch can instantly calm our mood and increase those feel-good hormones which include oxytocin, dopamine, and serotonin. Once these hormones are released into our bodies, we experience feelings of happiness, relaxation, and lower levels of depression—making it easier to manage all of our responsibilities.

EVENING SELF-CARE IDEAS
Exercise
There are so many great exercise options, but it is important to find something that works well for you, your personality, your schedule, and your goals! You can try anything from high intensity group fitness classes, to yoga in your living room. We are all different in so many ways, so don't get discouraged if you try something and end up hating it—just try something else.

Ask yourself the following questions to help narrow down exercise options that might work for you personally: Do I like to exercise by myself, with a friend, or in a group? Do I prefer to workout at a gym or at home? Do I like high, moderate, or low intensity workouts? Do I like exercise that is more recreational, like swimming or playing tennis? How much time do I have to dedicate to exercise each week? Where will my kids be while I'm exercising? Find a routine that works for you. Carving out this time to focus on your own physical and mental health can benefit you in more ways than one.

Turn off Your Phone
Once my whole family is home in the evening, I purposefully turn my phone to silent and put it in another room to charge for an hour or more. This gives me quality time to focus on the people in front of me without any other distractions. I am able to be productive and connect with my family, without feeling pulled in so many different directions. And once my phone is out of sight and out of mind, I instantly start to feel calmer.

Of course, I am realistic about these expectations and purposeful with how I implement this into my own routine. Our jobs and our kids' activities often require us to stay tuned in and up to date on what is going on, which is why my phone is beside me for the majority of each day. But I encourage you to carve out small windows of time to reset and recharge—both your phone and yourself.

Snuggle
Evenings can be a busy time for families. We spend our time trying to feed everyone dinner, check backpacks, complete homework, run back and forth to activities, and get stuff ready for the following day. In the midst of all of that, it

is easy to forget to reconnect with our loved ones. Physical closeness can really help us feel loved because it is not something that we share with many people!

I love to end each evening wrapped up in a cozy blanket with a glass of something calming, while sitting on the couch with my husband or one of my littles beside me. My favorite thing is being able to cuddle up as a family on our big sectional sofa and watch a family game show or a movie together. And when that isn't doable on a weeknight, we try for smaller snuggly moments that still allow us to relax before bedtime. The important thing is that you make the effort to be present in the moment and appreciate the love that you have right there around you!

My hope is that this list of ideas inspires you to find more ways to check in with yourself throughout your crazy days. Find things that relax, energize, and inspire you. What keeps you moving in a positive direction on a daily basis? Once you start making this extra effort for yourself, you will see how much more you actually have to give!

*

Connect with Your Kids: Prepare for Summer Fun

The days are getting longer, the weather is warmer, and summer is right around the corner. For many kids (and adults), it's their favorite time of the year. It is so refreshing to get out of the house, take a break from school, and enjoy everything that the outdoors has to offer. Whether your family prefers camping in the mountains or building sand castles at the beach, you will likely find yourself around water over these next few months. And while a pool day is always enjoyable, child safety needs to be at the top of our minds as we begin venturing out and about.

Every summer the kids are a little older and a little more independent. They like to push the limits and see what new things they can try this year. They might be at the age where they start experimenting with going underwater, jumping in without their floaties, or diving off of the diving board. By the end of the summer, they will have mastered some new skill! But at the start of the summer, we need to be extra cautious as we all navigate new abilities and interests for the first time.

Because I have several children that can't get enough of the water (I swear they were born with gills), I had to come up with a routine to ensure that everyone stays safe, and we can continue to enjoy our water days. Below is our daily routine when heading to our community pool. And with a little tweaking, it can also be applied to water parks, lakes, rivers, and beaches.

Know Your Limits

My biggest piece of advice for parents is to know your limits. We all want to be that parent that handles a day at the pool with ease, but it requires a lot of preparation, patience, and energy to make that happen. Just like when you're at home, you never quite know what the day will bring. How will you manage if someone needs to be fed, someone else needs to go to the bathroom, and someone refuses to get out of the water? You are only one person!

As parents we want to do it all and prefer not to always ask for, or pay for, extra help. However, the water can be a dangerous place for any little ones that are not properly supervised, so water safety for our kids has to be our top priority! After my second and third kids were each born, I never went to the pool without help from a family member, friend, or babysitter. Whether they came along to be an extra set of eyes and hands, or if they kept my baby at home, I knew I couldn't go to the pool with all three of my kids—all by myself—until they were a little older.

Prepare Ahead of Time

It is tough to leave the house when you have little ones. I would often have to start planning to leave the house at least an hour before we needed to be anywhere. But when you are repeatedly going to the same place (like the neighborhood pool), you can prepare ahead of time. I always keep a separate pool bag in the closet beside the towels. It is stocked with sunscreen, goggles, Band-Aids, bug repellent, ziplock bags (for wet or dirty items), tissues, a hairbrush, and hair ties. Then when we want to go to the pool, I throw in sunglasses, hats, a change of dry clothes, a few snacks, and water bottles.

I have a shelf right by my car in the garage where I keep our seasonal gear. In the summertime, this shelf holds the puddle jumpers, pool floats, and a toy bag with sand and water toys. Keeping a separate summer bag of toys keeps my kids from collecting things around the house that would then need to be cleaned and returned. It keeps these toys fun and exciting as well because they only use them when we're out and about.

We also put on bathing suits and apply sunscreen at home. It is much easier to help all of the kids get ready in our own home, instead of in a public changing area, and allows more time for the sunscreen to absorb into their skin before getting wet. And most kids want to hurry into the water as soon as possible after arriving, so you don't have to try to delay the fun once you get there!

Be Careful of Rafts

There is a reason that many swimming areas do not allow rafts. And while we don't want to scare anyone, it is important to know the potential dangers of seemingly harmless water activities. I am extremely careful anytime my kids are playing with rafts in the pool after a dear friend had a scary experience. Her daughter is a strong swimmer, but one time she got trapped under a large pool raft. Every time she tried to pop up for air, she was still under the raft. The lifeguard could not see what was happening underneath and did not know that she was struggling. Thankfully, her dad noticed and jumped in and saved her (with all of his clothes on). It is a crucial reminder that we *always* have to keep an eye on our kids when they're in the water, and to be cautious around rafts and other potentially dangerous objects.

Be Clear and Consistent

On our way to the pool I remind my children of what behaviors are appropriate, and how I expect our pool trip to go. I make it clear that if we are not playing in the water safely and following the rules, we will leave immediately. It is a simple, yet effective natural consequence that encourages everyone to cooperate. Your kids may test your boundaries on this point, which is only natural. But it typically only takes one or two times of following through on your word, packing up, and leaving the pool for them to understand that you are taking things seriously.

It is also important to stay calm throughout these situations. Packing up and leaving early in a calm, collected manner is much more effective than yelling at your kids in the hopes that it will change their behavior. You can ignore the whining and pleading, stay steadfast in the fact that you're going back home, and let them know that they can try again another day.

Pool Day Routine

Since we go to the pool so often, we have a routine that we follow each time. (Print out a visual pool day checklist to help your kids learn the routine.)

- As we get out of the car, I give each child something to carry. This helps to prevent them from jumping in before we arrive at our usual spot.
- Once we get to our chairs, everyone takes off their cover-ups and puts them in our waterproof pool bag so we don't have wet clothes later.
- All of the sandals go under my chair.
- I help put on puddle jumpers, swimmies, floaties, or whatever they're using.
- Once I give them the okay, they are allowed to go sit on the pool steps or in the shallow end while I lay out our towels and other pool day items.
- After I finish setting up our space, I give the kids the thumbs-up to go swim!

The kids know what to expect each time, and I don't have to feel frazzled or worried at any step of the process. I can relax and focus on them having fun for the rest of the time.

While I might sound a little strict, planning ahead, being organized, and reviewing our plan with the kids has saved a lot of time, mishaps, and frustration. Please do not think that my children are perfect little robots that always follow each step exactly, because they are still kids who on occasion have their challenging moments. But I have found that it's much easier to get them back on track when there is a sense of order from the start. They learned from an early age that following my guidelines at the pool is a lot more fun than having to leave abruptly and head back home for naps or quiet time.

I follow routines and think through potential safety hazards so that we can make the most of our summers. Even older children and teenagers need clear instructions and open conversations about water safety. You don't need to scare them, but you do need them to be aware that they aren't invincible, and it can be helpful for them to know what to do in different situations. Since we now live on the coast, I hear about injuries or even deaths involving teenagers and young adults way too often. While every situation is different, it is a constant reminder to always prepare your kids, use caution, and teach them how to be responsible around water at any age. Summertime is meant to be fun and exciting. Just make sure you are all enjoying it safely!

*

Work from Home: Maintain Your Productivity

In an ideal world, you'd be able to settle in at your desk and get into a flow state—a focused rhythm. However, the reality of working from home with kids is that you have constant interruptions. You have to adapt and figure out how to maintain your productivity in smaller bursts.

This isn't necessarily a bad thing. Kids force us to take breaks, stand up and stretch our legs, look away from the computer, remember that there are more important things in life, and provide us with comic relief throughout the day. As we discussed on page 9, adjusting our expectations can make a world of difference. And once we begin to accept that our work will have to be done in sprints throughout each day, we can be purposeful about what that looks like.

I have always been a scheduler. I like things planned out. I like things to happen at certain times on certain days. But the moment that I became a parent, that all had to change. My adorable little baby would cry anytime we weren't nursing or walking. Things only started to get better when I let go of my rigid thinking, gave up the idea of any sort of schedule, and learned to be present in the moment.

This still holds true today—even as my children get older. When they need me, I shift my attention to them. When they are playing happily, I sit down at the computer and work like crazy. I have also realized the value in being physically present for them even while working on something else. It's not a perfect system. I don't have set hours. I work when I can and try not to get too frustrated when I can't. And despite the ebb and flow of working from home, I keep my kids happy and healthy while also meeting deadlines.

Take Advantage of Your Smartphone

Smartphones have come a long way since the days of having to press the number "7" four times to type the letter "S." My smartphone has allowed me to write articles while holding a sleeping baby on the beach, update websites while keeping an eye on my kids at the playground, and answer phone calls while paddle boarding at the lake. Yes, always being plugged in to your smartphone can be detrimental, but it can also be extremely freeing!

Instead of feeling like we need to be tied to our desk, we are able to go out into the world. I am able to maintain productivity and a fun work-life balance thanks to my smartphone. I am able to let my kids run around and enjoy the fresh air at a playground without worrying that I'll miss an important email. I can take them to the library and let them play and explore while using the Wi-Fi to get some work done. Of course, there are jobs and tasks that require you to be at your desk at certain hours, but if you have some freedom and flexibility, make sure you are taking advantage of that!

There are also tons of apps that allow us to do incredible things with our smartphones. We can scan documents, edit pictures and videos, design graphics, use speech-to-text features, and so much more. These can be great time-savers, but make sure that you aren't overcomplicating things for yourself. Keep it simple!

Create a Five Minute To-Do List

Being a parent often means that you have weird chunks of time when you are simply waiting for your kids to need something. You have five minutes before you have to leave to pick your child up from soccer practice. You have ten minutes before you need to start the bedtime routine. You have three minutes in the pickup line before the school bell rings. What do you currently do with those small windows of time? Many of us are guilty of wasting away those precious minutes scrolling through social media when we could be doing something more meaningful with our time.

You can create your own five minute to-do list with items that are very specific to you. Figure out which work tasks only take a few moments of your time and add them to the list so that you can easily reference it the next time you have a couple of free minutes.

Five Minute To-Do List Ideas

Instead of letting those minutes tick by, create a five minute to-do list for yourself. Ideas for this to-do list can include:

1. Reply to emails that won't require much of your time.
2. Bookmark articles that you want to read later and revisit them when you have a few spare moments.
3. Text a friend to let them know you're thinking of them.
4. Close your eyes and take a few deep breaths.
5. Create a to-do list for the rest of your day or week.
6. Do a few yoga or stretching exercises.
7. Unload the dishwasher (I promise it only takes a few minutes even though it feels much longer).
8. Make up a silly story with your kids.
9. Read a few pages of a book.
10. Complete other work tasks that only take a few moments.

We firmly believe in the importance of downtime and self-care, and you certainly don't have to schedule every minute of every day. However, we do want you to be aware of where you are wasting precious time. It is much more freeing and relaxing to complete that small work task than to spend the rest of the day thinking about it. It is much more fulfilling to text a friend or laugh with your child than to mindlessly scroll through your phone. The point of this to-do list is simply to keep you aware of your time and moving forward in a productive way.

Stop Trying So Hard

Working from home can sometimes feel like trying to put a square peg into a round hole. No matter how hard you try, things won't fall into place. Instead of beating yourself up about this, step back, regroup, and change something. There are many people that try to tell you that rigid schedules are the secret to productivity, but I have a feeling those people aren't parents. For me, personally, the key to work-at-home productivity as a parent is being purposeful with each moment that I have. I love when my family seems to settle into a routine with some consistency. It is magical to feel like the days ebb and flow with some regularity. But I have also been doing this parenting thing long enough to know that those routines can change overnight. And instead of mourning the loss of my great routine, or fighting against the current to try to get it back, I have simply learned to adjust to a new normal—whatever that may be.

There have been seasons of my life when I mostly worked in the evenings because the kids were little and needed almost constant attention. I would do small tasks throughout the day and then dive into the more focused tasks once my husband could take over. There have been seasons when most of my focused work took place early in the day so that I could be present for my kids once they got home from school and before they were off to their activities. And there have been seasons of my life when the work had to happen throughout the day whenever the opportunity presented itself, being drawn back to my computer when an important email notification would come through, and working alongside my kids as they navigated virtual learning.

Once we stop trying so hard to control every aspect of our lives, we are able to spend that energy on the tasks at hand. There is a lot that we need to let go of so that productivity can become a priority again.

*

Monthly Reflections

Since parenting requires so much from us day after day, it can be hard to slow down and take the time to reflect on what's working and what we need to change. You might be tempted to breeze past these monthly checkpoints, but we highly recommend that you take a few minutes to stop and reflect on the past month while it's still fresh in your mind.

There are a few reasons to do this exercise each month. First of all, it encourages you to live and parent more mindfully. It is a checkpoint so that you don't continue on the same path month after month, year after year. If something isn't working well for you and your family, you have the opportunity to identify that and begin to correct it!

It also gives you the opportunity to highlight and appreciate the things that *are* going well. Feeling gratitude for amazing people and moments in your life will lead to even more positivity in the following month. We want to train our brains to see the bright side, and monthly reflections are a simple way to do that.

Once you work through your monthly reflections, you may want to share your thoughts with trusted loved ones in your life. It is a great way to share insight with your partner, your coworkers, and your friends. You can share new ideas with them, and they will be able to support you moving forward as well!

May
Monthly Reflections

Five Highlights
What were your favorite moments from the month?

_____

_____

_____

Four Things You Focused on
What took up the most brain power this month?

_____

_____

_____

Three Game Changers
What were those a-ha moments?

_____

_____

_____

Two Things You Didn't Get to
Do you need to get to them next month?

_____

_____

_____

One Disappointment

Did you take time to grieve that moment?

_____

_____

_____

Next Month

What do you want to continue for the next month?

_____

_____

_____

What do you want to change for the next month?

_____

_____

Notes

_____

_____

_____

_____

_____

_____

_____

_____

_____

_____

_____

Chapter 6
June

This month signals the end of the school year and brings us Father's Day. This chapter highlights and appreciates the unique abilities dads offer while parenting. We share parenting advice for helping siblings get along now that they will be spending more time together. And we provide encouragement for setting boundaries and taking time away from your work.

*

Monthly Intentions

At the beginning of each month, we'll leave space for you to prioritize, plan, and prepare. As parents, our lives can start to feel like a series of small emergencies. One simple way to keep things organized is to set clear priorities and plan accordingly for the month ahead. Answering these five questions at the start of each month only takes a few minutes, but it will help you feel organized and ready to tackle the next thirty days.

Note: Daily and weekly plans are a great way to make sure that you are maintaining your monthly priorities and staying focused. Free printable planners can also be found on our website: AdoreThemParenting.com/Book-Resources.

June
Monthly Intentions

1. What are some things that I can do to improve my own well-being?

   _____

   _____

   _____

2. How can I support and connect with my partner?

   _____

   _____

   _____

3. What do my kids need me to make a priority?

   _____

   _____

   _____

4. What will I need to focus on for work?

   _____

   _____

   _____

5. Which household tasks or projects need my attention?

   _____

   _____

   _____

Focus on You: Appreciate and Celebrate Dads

As we get ready to celebrate Father's Day, we want to take the time to appreciate these important loved ones. Whether you spend this holiday celebrating your children's father, your own father, or another important father figure in your life, the same sentiment applies—dads have a unique role in our lives!

Active Fun

While moms are superheroes in our own way, dads tend to take the active play to a whole new level. I love that my kids have someone in their lives that will happily run around on the playground, carry them on his shoulders, play the rough-and-tumble games, throw them into the pool, go on bike rides, set up sprinklers, and take the lead on any of these types of energetic activities. While I still like to join in on the craziness from time to time, it's nice to know that my husband will lead the charge in this area. And when it's time to wind down and switch to a calmer activity, then it's my time to shine.

Fresh Patience

Being a work-from-home mom is incredibly exhausting. The demands are constant throughout each and every day, and I am often counting down the minutes until my husband walks through the front door. I know I am very lucky to have this type of partner, and I don't take that lightly. When Dad gets home he has a fresh amount of patience for the kids and is ready to switch gears from work-mode to dad-mode. This gives me the flexibility to do my own thing, at least for a little while!

Rational Perspective

I don't want to overgeneralize, but at least in my relationship, I am the more emotional one. I am the one that can spiral into negative thoughts more quickly than my husband, and I am the one that has a harder time letting go of minor mishaps. I am so appreciative of the objective, rational, and steadying perspectives of the men in my life. They are able to be supportive, yet realistic. And they can step up and be that voice of reason when I need them to be.

20 Activities to Connect with Dad

1. Grill together
2. Work on a school project
3. Clean out the garage
4. Learn how to fix something
5. Detail the car
6. Build something together
7. Plan a surprise for the family
8. Exercise together
9. Run errands
10. Do yard work
11. Play sports
12. Go fishing
13. Play laser tag
14. Ride bikes
15. Play a card game
16. Fly kites
17. Go bowling
18. Build a fort
19. Go out for ice cream
20. Play at the park

Family Protector

Late one night, we heard loud noises that sounded like someone was trying to break into our house. I have never seen anyone grab a baseball bat and sprint toward the "danger" so fast. Thankfully, it turned out that a shelf had collapsed. Everything on it had fallen to the ground, so there wasn't any real danger. But that moment showed me that Dad was ready and willing to protect his family. The way that fathers fight for their families is an incredible thing to see and appreciate.

Sense of Humor

My kids love that Dad is always ready with a funny story or a silly joke when they need some distraction. He keeps the kids entertained on long car rides, lovingly teases everyone at family gatherings, and brings a smile to my face when I'm taking life too seriously. I love that the dads in my life seem to have kept a little bit of their boyish mischief and are able to keep our days fun and interesting!

Know-It-All

There seems to be a dad thing where over the years, they gradually become a jack-of-all-trades. One house project at a time, they turn into a resident handyman who always wants to at least try to fix something before calling the professionals. They also seem to collect small tidbits of pointless knowledge. They know a lot about a lot, and you never know when they'll chime in with a little-known piece of trivia. Maybe it is because they never want to admit that they don't know something, or more positively . . . maybe it's because they have a great capacity to learn these types of things. Either way, we're always happy to have them around!

Little Moments

I also appreciate that my husband makes the most of mundane moments. It is easy to get caught up in our normal everyday routines, but he is quick to make even a normal weeknight fun. If the kids want to make s'mores, he happily makes a fire in the backyard. If it's his turn to tuck the kids into bed, he'll turn old stories into new silly versions. If he has to run to the store, he'll turn it into a fun mission with the children. Those little moments are the things that our kids will remember most when they look back on their childhood, and they don't go unnoticed.

So here's a big "Thank You!" to the father figures in our lives. Thank you for being larger than life. Thank you for being our rock. Thank you for being so selfless. Thank you for being *you*.

*

Connect with Your Kids: Help Siblings Get Along

Now that school is wrapping up, your kids will likely be spending a lot more time together at home. While it is nice to have a break from the morning marathon of getting everyone up and ready for school on time, this season can present its own challenges. How do you keep everyone entertained and getting along? How do you create respectful boundaries that allow each person to have some personal space when needed?

It's a tricky balance. But it can be done. Consider using this summer to help your children strengthen their bond with one another. Every child is unique and has different interests, but the goal is to help our kids appreciate their differences while also finding some common ground. Getting along with siblings is a great life lesson in figuring out how to get along with friends, classmates, and even coworkers down the road. So it is worth the extra effort to work through potential issues and help siblings get along with each other now.

While I know that my children love each other very much, sometimes it takes a little extra encouragement and guidance to make it all run smoothly. Especially when they haven't spent as much time together recently. The start of summer can bring more sibling arguments as they are figuring out how to all get along for extended periods of time again. I always try to remember that in a few weeks, they will all be best friends once again. But those first few days of any school break (summer break or winter break) tend to bring out the sibling rivalry.

There is an ongoing conversation in our house about friendships, and how those same principles apply to our own siblings. While some friends will be in your life for a long time, others will come and go. However, your family will always be here. No matter what you do, your siblings will always be your siblings. And that simple fact is why it is so important that we respect and love one another—even when your brother is being objectively annoying.

Provide Bonding Opportunities

Each of my kids is very different. They have different talents, interests, and personality traits; and it is important for them to be able to grow up as their own, unique person. But it is also important that they learn the values of teamwork, compromise, and empathy. With a little support from you, kids are able to work on these important skills while playing with their siblings. (You can also use the Letter to My Sibling printable from AdoreThemParenting.com/Book-Resources to encourage kindness between your kids.)

Play is so important! And we can challenge ourselves to give our kids the space and tools they need to learn through their play. I try to provide plenty of space for them to run around outside together exploring nature, riding bikes, and taking turns playing each kid's favorite sport. And I make an effort to fill their playroom with toys that allow for multi-person creative play where they can team up and work together to bring their ideas to life.

Working together and helping each other is a key element of establishing sibling bonds. I try to put an emphasis on my older ones looking out for and helping the younger ones. However, helping their siblings does not mean that they become the parent. We talk a lot about their role as brother or sister, and what that means within the family. There are certain responsibilities that they can take on that will help the family as a whole, but there are also lines that are not helpful to cross. The kids don't make or even enforce the rules, but they can be great role models! And more often than not, the kids love seeing themselves as a team as we go out into the world.

When everyone is getting along, these scenarios can provide hours of entertaining fun. And when disagreements arise, it provides the perfect teaching opportunity on how to get along with others. Our children are learning what it means to respect other people's feelings, other people's property, how to compromise, how to share, and how to be a kind person that others want to play with. Imagine how this will benefit them for their future!

Allow Personal Space
It's also important to acknowledge that sometimes your kids will need a break from each other. I have one child who prefers to play with someone about 90 percent of the time, but that other 10 percent of the time, he wants to be completely alone. This was something that we had to figure out after plenty of meltdowns and numerous conversations. My son was able to get along with other kids, but he also needed breaks from the noise, activity, and overall stimulation.

We quickly realized that encouraging him to simply walk away and take a little break before he got too overwhelmed made a world of difference. During these breaks, he's not in trouble, but he might need some extra help creating a relaxing environment. He will often choose to go to his room, spread out on his floor, and play something quietly on his own. This downtime gives him a reset, and he is able to emerge from his room on his own feeling much happier and ready to play again.

The other piece of this puzzle is that his siblings have had to learn how to be respectful of this time too. They initially wanted to follow him, ask him what was wrong, try to fix things, or bug him. These attempts were, unsurprisingly, met with further arguments and meltdowns. We worked on everyone agreeing to respect his space, and he will even hang a sign on his door letting everyone know that he prefers to be alone so that we can avoid unpleasant interruptions while he is trying to unwind.

Walking away and taking time to cool down and decompress is a wonderful coping mechanism that will be beneficial for the rest of their lives.

Many of us adults could use work in this area as well! It's always a good idea to identify our own struggles, carve out space to deal with them, figure out appropriate coping tools, and respect other people's boundaries.

Appreciate the Benefits

Because my children are close, they genuinely care for one another. And now that three of my children are older and in elementary school, they love experiencing things together, creating fun memories, and sharing in special moments. Whether it is my daughter's soccer game, my son's football game, a swim meet, or even just finding a (supposedly) cute lizard in the backyard, they love being able to cheer each other on and discover new things together.

My husband and I have tried something different recently. Over the summer, we became a lot more relaxed in the evenings with the bedtime routine. Because we both work from home, and our kids stay home with us over the summer break, we are able to be a bit more lenient with our schedules.

Each night after dinner and showers, our three older kids will run upstairs to play in their bedrooms with each other. Every night they play something different, and they take turns picking what they will get into next. We eventually call them downstairs for bedtime snacks, and then they'll take their iPads back upstairs where they all log onto a game they can play together. As of writing this, they are building a city together, and it makes me so happy to hear them plan, talk through their ideas, and giggle the whole way through the process. Once it's time for lights out, they have been having "sibling sleepovers" where they all cuddle in the same big bed in our daughter's room. They break out their favorite pillows, blankets, and stuffed animals, and we can hear them whispering and giggling until they drift off to sleep.

The added bonus to all of this is that my husband and I get to spend a lot of quality time together too. We are able to have conversations without interruptions, watch our favorite shows together, and reconnect most evenings. And we are able to do all of that without arranging, paying, and cleaning up for a babysitter!

I understand that this may not work well for you, your family, and your current stage of life. But it is an example of how we can go with the flow and appreciate the hard work that we put into this whole parenting gig!

My children's sibling bonds are so incredibly special, and I take the task of helping them get along very seriously. I have these early years to try to cement that bond before they continue to pursue their individual interests and groups of friends. And I will continue to make it my mission to teach them how to be best friends that know how to fight fair and respect each other's differences.

I want my kids to have each other as a support system for the rest of their lives. I want them to be able to turn to each other when life throws them curveballs. And I want them to be able to reminisce on their childhood, and their crazy parents, decades from now.

*

Work from Home: Recognize and Address Burnout

We talk about self-care throughout this book, and the reason that we give these ideas so much value is that they truly matter. When self-care is lacking, everything else can feel like it's falling apart. And when you have neglected your own needs for too long, a candlelit bath seems like a Band-Aid instead of a real solution.

When you have reached this point, it often means that you are struggling with burnout. Which is totally understandable considering you are a parent who is working from home and faced with a huge amount of 24-7 tasks. There is no clocking in and clocking out. Despite your best plans, you never quite know what the day might bring. And despite all of the chaos, each day can feel strangely monotonous.

So what can we do?

Recognize the Signs of Burnout

The first step is to recognize the signs of burnout. Burnout is much more common than most of us realize, and it is much more serious than we might expect. Our culture glorifies busyness and pushing ourselves to the brink of collapse. If you are going through your life frantically jumping from one task to another without any time for reflection or relaxation, you are on the quick path to burning out.

The symptoms of burnout are caused by being in an ongoing state of stress. (Sound familiar?) And it grabs a hold of you by taking over the smaller things in your life. Simple things like replying to an email or packing lunches can start to feel daunting. General burnout symptoms can include feeling emotionally and/or physically exhausted, experiencing detachment and cynicism, and worrying that you're ineffective or unaccomplished.

That brief overview hit me hard the first time I read it. It felt like I was able to look at my life from an entirely different angle. Constantly questioning my own parenting methods or feeling like I needed some separation from my own children was not a sign of being a bad mom. It was a sign that I was burnt out. I would worry about not being able to reach my career goals and consistently felt like I was not meeting my potential even though rationally I knew that I was moving in the right direction. The feelings of self-doubt and exhaustion that would permeate my days also pointed to burnout.

Symptoms of burnout include the following:

- Feeling a sense of dread about what the day has in store for you.
- Experiencing physical symptoms like headaches, palpitations, and others.
- Feeling drained and tired most of the time.
- Struggling with insomnia despite feeling tired.
- Becoming more forgetful or having trouble staying focused.
- Feeling more worried or irritable than usual.
- Having increased feelings of guilt.
- Tending to be more pessimistic than usual.
- Shutting yourself off from others and becoming less social.
- Ignoring tasks and avoiding things you should be doing.

For many of us, this short list sounds all too familiar. The severity of what we are experiencing can and will vary. But at any stage, burnout is important to address. These signs tend to creep up on us slowly so that we begin to accept them as a part of normal, everyday life. The goal is to recognize these signs early before you get to a darker and more difficult place. I know. I know. Easier said than done. But keep reading . . .

Recover from Burnout

As soon as you start to recognize these signs within yourself, you should take action. We tend to think that we should power through and make things work, but sometimes taking a step back from it all can be the best remedy. Figuring out what you truly need is an important step in this process, and here are four key areas to consider when brainstorming ways to restore your sense of energy and excitement.

Rest/Relaxation: As parents, there is a good chance that you are genuinely tired! Your body and/or mind might be completely drained, which means that the only path to feeling better is taking the time to rest. Take the time to nap, watch a movie, read a book, take a bath, or listen to music. Allow yourself to slow down, be patient, and listen to what your body is telling you. Even going to bed earlier than usual for a few nights in a row can make a huge difference!

Companionship: When was the last time that you truly connected with a fellow human being? You might be craving that close human connection beyond quick chats on Zoom, via text, or at the grocery store. Schedule time to call a friend, coordinate dinner with a group of friends, text people that you haven't touched base with in a while, or write a love note to your partner. Our digital world allows us to always feel connected without diving deeper into those relationships so sometimes we have to make the effort to fill that empty bucket within ourselves.

Creativity/Expression: Work-from-home parents face a weird type of monotony. We long for the days when we had enough downtime to feel bored. We wish for just a few days when there isn't some sort of curveball. And yet, we aren't able to break free of our rigid schedules and routines. Juggling work and kids every day doesn't allow much time for creative expression. However, it is important to unwind and follow your own passions from time to time. These activities don't have to be time-consuming to be restorative! Simply take a few minutes to draw a picture, follow a writing prompt, sing karaoke in your living room, take pictures around town, or pursue other hobbies that you have long forgotten about.

Health/Spirituality: When we get busy, we tend to ignore our physical and mental health. Taking the time to move our bodies and quiet our minds can be hugely beneficial. Next time you have that antsy feeling, make it a priority to go for a walk, do a YouTube yoga video, meditate or pray, make yourself a healthy snack, or write down positive affirmations. Focusing on your overall wellness can help bring you back from the brink of burnout.

Plan a Trip
While the tips above are helpful in getting you through the daily grind, it can also be nice to schedule an actual break. There are, of course, limitations to this such as childcare, finances, health, or a big work project. But substantial breaks are very restorative when you can make them happen.

A Night Away: If you don't have anyone to watch the kids, consider taking a night to yourself. Have your partner stay with the children while you check into a hotel, stay at a friend's house, or lock yourself in the bedroom. Even just one night can feel luxurious if there are zero things you have to do.

A Day Trip: Most of us can manage to take a single day away from our work, and you can pack a lot of family fun into one day! Do some research, plan ahead, set up some auto-replies, and make the most of a family day completely unplugged from work.

Weekend Getaway: Leave the kids with someone you trust like a grandparent, relative, or friend, and get away with your partner or close friend for a weekend of downtime. Use this time to reconnect without any interruptions or distractions.

Family Vacation: Going somewhere new is fun and builds incredible memories. There is so much value in teaching your kids about a new area and providing everyone with new experiences. A family vacation can be rewarding, calming, and a way to bring everyone closer together.

While taking exotic trips abroad sounds amazing, it is not always possible. And sometimes those vacations even need a follow-up vacation after you are home from all of that travel and sightseeing. It's okay to rethink your vacations and adventures with the sole purpose of walking away from work for a while, taking a break from the duties around the house, and truly relaxing. The point of this break is to help you recover so that you can continue operating at your best.

Give Yourself Credit

Working from home means that much of our work goes unnoticed. Parenting our children also requires tons of work that goes unnoticed. And maintaining a home on top of all of that also goes unnoticed. We are in a thankless line of work, but that doesn't make it any less important. You are doing amazing things each and every day—even if you never get the credit you deserve.

In order to prove this to yourself, take the time to write down *all* of your responsibilities. Every tiny little thing that you keep in your head and manage for yourself, your family, your friends, your community, and your work. Get it all down on paper. Doing this simple task will help you realize how much you do on a daily, weekly, and monthly basis. You will start to understand why you are feeling overwhelmed and on the edge of total burnout.

Simply acknowledging this stress can be therapeutic in and of itself. But don't let it stop there. You get to be in control of your own life! You get to call the shots and make changes as needed. Keep recognizing the signs of burnout and take steps to avoid its more severe effects because the world needs you functioning at your best!

*

Monthly Reflections

Since parenting requires so much from us day after day, it can be hard to slow down and take the time to reflect on what's working and what we need to change. You might be tempted to breeze past these monthly checkpoints, but we highly recommend that you take a few minutes to stop and reflect on the past month while it's still fresh in your mind.

There are a few reasons to do this exercise each month. First of all, it encourages you to live and parent more mindfully. It is a checkpoint so that you don't continue on the same path month after month, year after year. If something isn't working well for you and your family, you have the opportunity to identify that and begin to correct it!

It also gives you the opportunity to highlight and appreciate the things that *are* going well. Feeling gratitude for amazing people and moments in your life will lead to even more positivity in the following month. We want to train our brains to see the bright side, and monthly reflections are a simple way to do that.

Once you work through your monthly reflections, you may want to share your thoughts with trusted loved ones in your life. It is a great way to share insight with your partner, your coworkers, and your friends. You can share new ideas with them, and they will be able to support you moving forward as well!

June
Monthly Reflections

Five Highlights
What were your favorite moments from the month?

_____

_____

_____

Four Things You Focused on
What took up the most brain power this month?

_____

_____

_____

Three Game Changers
What were those a-ha moments?

_____

_____

_____

Two Things You Didn't Get to
Do you need to get to them next month?

_____

_____

_____

One Disappointment

Did you take time to grieve that moment?

_____

_____

_____

Next Month

What do you want to continue for the next month?

_____

_____

_____

What do you want to change for the next month?

_____

_____

_____

Notes

_____

_____

_____

_____

_____

_____

_____

_____

_____

Chapter 7
July

Summer is in full swing, and we want to make the most of it! This chapter highlights ways that you can cut back, simplify, and enjoy the present moment with your family. We provide tips to help you plan and prepare for youth sports registration. And we share outside-the-box childcare ideas to help you through summer break and beyond.

*

Monthly Intentions

At the beginning of each month, we'll leave space for you to prioritize, plan, and prepare. As parents, our lives can start to feel like a series of small emergencies. One simple way to keep things organized is to set clear priorities and plan accordingly for the month ahead. Answering these five questions at the start of each month only takes a few minutes, but it will help you feel organized and ready to tackle the next thirty days.

Note: Daily and weekly plans are a great way to make sure that you are maintaining your monthly priorities and staying focused. Free printable planners can also be found on our website: AdoreThemParenting.com/Book-Resources.

July
Monthly Intentions

1. What are some things that I can do to improve my own well-being?

   _____

   _____

   _____

2. How can I support and connect with my partner?

   _____

   _____

   _____

3. What do my kids need me to make a priority?

   _____

   _____

   _____

4. What will I need to focus on for work?

   _____

   _____

   _____

5. Which household tasks or projects need my attention?

   _____

   _____

   _____

*

Focus on You: Simplify Your Life

If you're like me, then you might be guilty of binge-watching one tiny house show after another. They are incredibly fascinating, and I am intrigued with seeing how other people pare down their lifestyles. Their simplicity is so appealing, and it has inspired me to dial my own life back to the basics even though we won't be moving into a tiny home anytime soon!

I commend these people for being able to sell, purge, and pare down their belongings to fit into a significantly smaller living space. If I wasn't married with four growing children and a bunch of fluffy pets, I might even consider joining the movement! However, I have realized that I don't have to move into a tiny house to pare down my life.

After several life-changing moments, I became almost obsessed with finding ways to simplify my family's life. Things that weren't a priority went out the window. My main focus, after caring for my family, was clearing out our belongings. Anything that hadn't been used in a while, didn't serve a purpose, or didn't bring us sentimental joy went out the door. I went through all of our belongings one closet, one room, one area at a time. I channeled my inner Marie Kondo and literally picked up each and every object in my home and asked myself, "Is this functional or valuable to me?"

In addition to simplifying our belongings, we also overhauled our schedule, our activities, and even downsized our house (although our new one certainly isn't a tiny home). These changes were needed in order to help us cope with a physical injury and traumatic events that affected our family. This shift in our life was extremely therapeutic.

Thankfully, several years later, life is pretty fantastic again. And what started out as a necessity to survive a few challenging months, became a new lifestyle. I loved our simplified way of life so much that we continue to be intentional about maintaining it as much as possible.

For more than ten years, I had spent an incredible amount of time doing tasks and housework that often seemed endless and pointless. Something in my life had to give, and for me it was the house and the "stuff" in it. Now there is so much less to clean, less to look at, less to organize, and less to worry about. I spend a lot more time running around outside with my kids and doing fun things daily for myself.

As the kids get older there are more and more opportunities for them to get involved in sports and extracurricular activities. However, we are selective and think through whether that particular opportunity is worth the investment of both money and valuable time. If we are going to spend an evening out of the house, then it needs to be beneficial in some way. Kids can easily burn out from being overscheduled, and there is a careful balance of staying busy, having fun, but not overdoing it.

I have found that simplicity is truly beautiful. Basics are much easier. Details can make things complicated. Other people, their opinions, and their expectations can be daunting.

Get Started

There are many benefits to dialing your life back to the basics, and you can simplify in a way that fits you and your family's needs. You don't have to move into a tiny house or live through a traumatic moment to pare down your life.

You can start right now, exactly where you are in your current home. Once you get started, it will start to snowball—in a positive way! Pretty soon you'll find yourself wanting to make over your entire life. You will be able to embrace what really matters most instead of cleaning clutter and giving your valuable time to unnecessary tasks.

In order to get started, you first need to shift your mindset. Look at this journey as an adventure, not a to-do list. There is no time limit. And there is no end to this task. Simplifying is not a one-and-done thing; it is a lifestyle change. There will always be adjustments to you and your family's schedule, and new things coming into your space. Once you do your initial purge, it will be much easier to maintain. And after a busy phase of life, remember to take some time to reset and go through your schedule and house once again. The following tips will help you to embrace simplicity so that you can stay focused on what truly matters.

Go Back to Basics

Clear your calendar. I realize that this is much easier said than done. There will always be things that you need to accomplish and commitments that you will need to keep. But if there are any engagements on your calendar that aren't necessary, cancel them! Create a clean slate, and then be very particular about what you commit to moving forward. When you start to panic or feel bad about clearing out your schedule, think through the benefits. You will be able to dedicate more focus and attention to your work and your relationships when there are fewer things draining you of both your energy and your time.

Clear your phone. Our phones and electronics are an amazing tool while working from home, but they can also be a big distraction. Try turning off all of your notifications for a little while, and then only turn back on the notifications that you really need. While I need notifications on for my work email, I chose to turn them off for my personal email. I no longer receive alerts from social media and instead check in every once in a while when I have some free time to get caught up. These things will vary based on what you need and prefer for your personal and professional communication, but you should try to lessen the amount of daily interruptions from your phone.

Clear your house. The goal is to go through your entire home, but only focus on one room at a time so you don't feel overwhelmed. Physically touch everything. If it does not serve a purpose, or bring you sentimental joy, consider passing it on. If you need some help, look online for a cleaning checklist or challenge. (We have one available for free at AdoreThemParenting.com/Book-Resources to help you get started.) Again, the key here is to remember that there is no deadline or time frame for this task. I did several rounds of decluttering my house over the course of a year. With each round it got easier, and I realized there was more that I was willing to part with. For some of us that are more sentimental by nature (like me), it takes a lot of time and practice. But I am fully confident that you can do it too!

Make some piles. While decluttering, I always had a few piles going. One for trash, one to give away, one to box up, and one for consignment. I took clothes, toys, accessories, and home decor to my local consignment shop and was happy to receive some extra money for those items. And I dropped off anything they didn't accept at a donation center on the way home. My rule though is that once something leaves my house, it is not coming back in! I also made a pile of things to give to friends or family members that would appreciate them and give them a good home.

After your house and schedule are overhauled, and you have truly dialed everything back to basics, breathe. Take some time for yourself. And be intentional as you slowly allow things back into your home and routine. Life is short, and you have every right to enjoy it! It can become overly complicated and cluttered quickly, especially if you have a hard time saying "No." It can throw us curveballs from time to time while trying to raise our family. But I try to live my life in a way that teaches my kids that hard moments don't stop us. We can always go back to basics, readjust, and move forward in a new way. We can grow stronger and learn valuable life lessons. And we can appreciate the beauty in simplicity.

*

Connect with Your Kids: Plan for Youth Sports

Encouraging your child to try a new sport or activity can be very beneficial! Not only can it provide an additional opportunity to get exercise; but mastering new skills, forming new friendships, and learning teamwork all have advantages. There are so many sports to choose from, and it's important to find the right fit for your child. Some offer team involvement, and others they can perform solo. Some can be played outdoors seasonally, and others are enjoyed year-round indoors.

When deciding on a new sport, start with your child's focus since there is probably already something that they are gravitating toward. Keep their age, maturity level, personality, and physical abilities in mind when making your selection. You can help pique their interest by taking them to a sporting event—even if it's the local high school team or a semi-pro event. The environment can be very exciting, and your kids will love seeing future potential for the sport if they stick with it. The goal is to give them a taste of what that sport requires, and a glimpse of the fun that they could have with it! Once your child shows some interest in a particular sport, your job doesn't end. There are plenty of questions that you as the parent will still need to ask and consider.

How Much Time Is Required?

Find out ahead of time what the schedule demands will be. The registration process alone can take a while between sign-ups, try-outs, evaluations, and so on. It's important to understand the time commitment before you start the process.

Find out the expectations and schedules for both practices and games. Some coaches require a certain amount of attendance, or your child might not receive playing time. Some coaches ask the kids to commit to practicing at home for an additional ten to twenty minutes per day as well. You'll need to be honest with yourself and your child. Are they ready for the added responsibility and discipline that comes along with this team? Are you able to realistically fit this activity into your family's weekly schedule?

The good thing is that there are typically many tiers of programs for a single sport. So while a more involved program might not be the right fit for your child or family as a whole this season, they may be able to play at a less intense level to continue to have fun and build skills.

How Safe Is This Sport?

Some sports are naturally safer than others. A full contact sport may bring more risk than a solo sport, but there are many other factors that go into ensuring the safety of young athletes. It is your job as a parent to do a little investigative work before signing your child up for a particular team. You can ask around, talk to other parents on the team, and even go watch a practice to get a feel for the environment. Before sports registration, here are some questions that you may want to consider . . .

- Does the coach do a good job of having the players follow the rules?
- Does the coach and league require the use of proper safety equipment?
- Do players take the time to warm up and cool down before and after each practice?
- In hot weather, does the coach pay attention to hydration, humidity, and temperature?
- Are children taught proper basics, movement, and body positioning?
- Is the coach attentive to the prevention and recognition of concussions?

What Is the Coaching Style?

Different kids respond to different coaching styles, and this one single factor can make or break your child's experience with the sport. The goal is to find a coach that will teach and challenge your young athlete, but in a positive and helpful way. Youth sports should be about fostering a love of the sport, building basic skills, and teaching life lessons such as resilience and the importance of a good work ethic. The reality is that kids grow and change throughout the years so the goal is to establish healthy building blocks in our children, rather than adopt a win-at-all-costs attitude that results in the kids burning out before they even reach high school.

Take the time to do your research in this area again, and when you find a great coach, hang on to them! Talk to fellow parents, get recommendations, and go watch practices. And if you get a bad gut feeling about a particular coach or club, listen to your instincts. You want your children to be in an environment that enhances their love of sports, not one that crushes their spirits.

Is This Right for My Kid?

It is important that you have an honest conversation with your child. Nowhere does it say that your child has to play sports. Maybe they enjoy drama, choir, playing instruments, or are really into creating artwork. Some children find their passion at a young age, and others need to try a variety of interests before discovering what they love. But whatever it is, ask yourself and your child these three important questions:

1. Is my child really enjoying or benefiting from this activity?
2. Is it worth the time that we are missing from being at home as a family?
3. Is my child handling the demands of his or her schedule both mentally and physically?

If the answers to these questions are "yes," then keep it going! And if the answer is "no," then there is nothing wrong with taking a little break and waiting a few weeks (or even years) before revisiting the options. There is no right or wrong answer for what age your child should be involved with activities. It all depends on your family, the child, and their personal interests.

*

Work from Home: Find Creative Childcare Options

When you work from home you need to get creative with how to keep your children entertained in order to be productive. Throughout this book, we have mentioned how beneficial it is to get your children set up with some activities before diving into your workload. However, sometimes you desperately need other options. While most of us would love to hire an au pair or a full-time nanny, those added costs are not always feasible. Or perhaps you only need help over the summer while school is out, which means that you'd prefer a more temporary solution.

One summer after having our third child, I hired someone to help out part-time. She came three days a week and just for a few hours while I remained in the home. If I was going to spend the money, I wanted to make sure that it really counted so I had her come late in the morning and stay through early afternoon. It seemed pointless to pay someone to be there while a child or two napped so I picked hours where everyone was usually awake. Having her there during lunchtime was also a big help because she agreed to prepare the food and sit with the kids while they ate. My only other request of her was that she would take the kids outside to play. The more active they were, the better the chance that I could get them to nap later, which stretched out my productivity even more. I was only paying for a few hours of childcare, but since I was strategic about it, I was able to continue working after she had left.

But before paying anyone, make sure you weigh the pros and cons. Hiring someone to help with the kids will shift your household budget, and it might require you to make some other changes within your home. Because of this financial commitment, you'll also want to make the most of your time while you have childcare! Do the things that require your full focus like a conference call, wrapping up a report, and other tasks that demand attention to detail. Save the less urgent tasks for later in the day when you can get them done in between helping the kids.

Hiring some extra help can be a great way to achieve your goals while still being budget-friendly. But if you're looking for some other creative childcare options, I've got you covered! Over the years of working from home, I've discovered some cost-effective and free ways to keep your kids safe and entertained while you get some work done.

Hire a Mother's Helper

Ask around your neighborhood or community to find out if anyone's older child is interested in being a mother's helper. Oftentimes these individuals are preteens who are looking for experience with the hope of one day becoming a babysitter. Typically these kids are not quite old enough to be left alone. And you may want to think twice if you have a small infant, unless you are willing to put in the time to help properly train them. But a mother's helper can be the perfect solution to finding someone to simply play with and entertain your children. I used to have a neighbor girl across the street who loved to do this. I never asked her to prepare a meal or do anything around the house. All I wanted was for her to keep my kids occupied in the playroom while I worked in another room. She would sit on the floor and play for hours with them! She charged half of what a normal sitter would charge, had fun with the kids, and gained a lot of valuable childcare experience. It's a great option for work-from-home parents who will still be able to supervise.

Use Your Gym

I used to belong to a gym that had a very nice large kid's club with a lot of adult supervision. For a minimal monthly fee, we could add our children onto our membership and give them access to the kid's club that included tunnels, slides, ball pits, a basketball court, and a room full of toys for the little ones. This allowed me to get a workout in if I wanted, and then sit in the café area with my laptop and get some work done before I picked them up. And because they had been running nonstop for two hours, they were usually ready for some quiet time once we returned home. Check with your local gyms, rec centers, and YMCAs to see what they offer. Some will even let you pay just for the day, which can help you out in a bind!

Enjoy Play Areas

Depending on your kids' ages and abilities, a fenced-in playground that has Wi-Fi access might work out nicely. They can play in a contained space while you get a little work done sitting on a nearby bench or picnic table as long as you are still supervising. Libraries, play areas at fast food restaurants, and even children's museums often offer Wi-Fi access and enclosed play areas. You won't be able to get hours' worth of work done in these locations, but you can absolutely squeeze in some productivity while your kids have fun.

Share a Sitter

Consider finding a neighbor or friend to split the cost of a sitter. You will want to limit the amount of kids involved in this type of arrangement and be considerate of the sitter's capabilities and experience. When my kids were little, this wasn't the best option for me; but now that they are in elementary school and fairly self-sufficient, I only need someone to oversee that everyone plays fairly, no one gets hurt, and that the meals are prepared. Adding a few more self-sufficient kids to the mix shouldn't overload the sitter, and then the parents can split the cost as well. Even if we pay a higher rate since there are more kids in the sitter's care, it still ends up costing less than if I paid for a sitter by myself. You and your friends can also take turns with offering your house as the host house for this childcare arrangement.

Join a Community Playgroup

Some neighborhoods may already have something like this organized, but if not, you could put one together. While this option might not allow you to get much work done, it can provide a free social outlet for everyone. In my old neighborhood, we had a group of five parents who all had kids around similar ages. We would take turns hosting a playgroup every few days, and whoever could make it would show up with their little ones. Us parents would get to chat while our kids got to enjoy playing in a different environment. While I would have felt rude sitting there on my laptop for the entire time, I did feel like I could step out of the room for a few minutes to take a work call or respond to a time-sensitive email because there were plenty of eyes on my children.

Take Turns Babysitting

This might not be your daily go-to, but it can be a good option every now and then. Ask a neighbor or friend to exchange childcare with you. One day you keep all of the kids at your house. And another day they can return the favor and keep all of the kids at their house. While this might not cost you any extra money, it does cost you in time. However, if you work part-time, this might be a perfect solution. And if you are swapping with someone that lives close by, or even down the street, you could swap partway through the day. Meaning one of you takes the morning shift and the other the afternoon shift.

While working from home with kids is a lot to juggle, it is just a phase. Eventually they will head off to school. Eventually they will become more independent and self-reliant. And eventually you will miss hearing, "Mommy, I need you!" So while it can be frustrating, try to make the most of it. My kids understand that at times work requires more of my time and concentration. But once I am through with that project or meet that deadline, I try extra hard to give my children my undivided attention. It is a constant balance. We won't get it right all of the time, but if our kids know that they are loved and valued, that's what is most important!

*

Monthly Reflections

Since parenting requires so much from us day after day, it can be hard to slow down and take the time to reflect on what's working and what we need to change. You might be tempted to breeze past these monthly checkpoints, but we highly recommend that you take a few minutes to stop and reflect on the past month while it's still fresh in your mind.

There are a few reasons to do this exercise each month. First of all, it encourages you to live and parent more mindfully. It is a checkpoint so that you don't continue on the same path month after month, year after year. If something isn't working well for you and your family, you have the opportunity to identify that and begin to correct it!

It also gives you the opportunity to highlight and appreciate the things that *are* going well. Feeling gratitude for amazing people and moments in your life will lead to even more positivity in the following month. We want to train our brains to see the bright side, and monthly reflections are a simple way to do that.

Once you work through your monthly reflections, you may want to share your thoughts with trusted loved ones in your life. It is a great way to share insight with your partner, your coworkers, and your friends. You can share new ideas with them, and they will be able to support you moving forward as well!

July
Monthly Reflections

Five Highlights
What were your favorite moments from the month?

_____

_____

_____

Four Things You Focused on
What took up the most brain power this month?

_____

_____

_____

Three Game Changers
What were those a-ha moments?

_____

_____

_____

Two Things You Didn't Get to
Do you need to get to them next month?

_____

_____

_____

One Disappointment

Did you take time to grieve that moment?

_____

_____

_____

Next Month

What do you want to continue for the next month?

_____

_____

_____

What do you want to change for the next month?

_____

_____

_____

Notes

_____

_____

_____

_____

_____

_____

_____

_____

Chapter 8
August

This month can be a difficult transition for families as summer comes to an end and kids head back to school. In this chapter, we provide practical tips to help parents find time for their well-being as the calendar fills up and expectations increase. We offer advice for helping kids start the school year with a positive outlook and helpful routines. And we focus on enjoying the many benefits that working from home has to offer.

*

Monthly Intentions

At the beginning of each month, we'll leave space for you to prioritize, plan, and prepare. As parents, our lives can start to feel like a series of small emergencies. One simple way to keep things organized is to set clear priorities and plan accordingly for the month ahead. Answering these five questions at the start of each month only takes a few minutes, but it will help you feel organized and ready to tackle the next thirty days.

Note: Daily and weekly plans are a great way to make sure that you are maintaining your monthly priorities and staying focused. Free printable planners can also be found on our website: AdoreThemParenting.com/Book-Resources.

August
Monthly Intentions

1. What are some things that I can do to improve my own well-being?

_____

_____

_____

2. How can I support and connect with my partner?

_____

_____

_____

3. What do my kids need me to make a priority?

_____

_____

_____

4. What will I need to focus on for work?

_____

_____

_____

5. Which household tasks or projects need my attention?

_____

_____

_____

*

Focus on You: Find Time for Wellness

When life gets busy, it can be so hard to keep the little, yet important things from falling through the cracks! We start to switch into survival mode where only the most crucial tasks get completed, and we are left feeling unfulfilled, out of touch, and guilty about all of the tasks that got put on the back burner for far too long. The reality is that life doesn't ever really slow down. We can't live our lives postponing things for the day when we aren't busy—because that day will never come.

There will always be another meal to cook, another appointment to schedule, another meeting to attend, another load of laundry to wash, another school form to sign, another big deadline to meet, another party to plan, another extracurricular to drive to, another email to answer, and so on . . .

Is it tough to juggle it all? Yes! But this is what we signed up for, and we can't throw in the towel. It is normal to have really tough days, weeks, or even months; but it is also important to at least try to find stress management solutions and better organize our lives. Staying on top of the smaller items is truly important to our health, happiness, relationships, and overall well-being! So what can we do about it?

We spend a lot of time throughout this book providing you with tips and strategies to manage working from home, parenting your kids, and finding time for yourself. But we also want you to feel better equipped to manage some of the other aspects of your life that tend to get neglected when life gets extra busy.

Spend Time with Friends

We can all agree that friendships and family relationships should not suffer when life gets crazy, but in reality, they often do. The good thing is that our true loved ones are patient with us, and they forgive us after we resurface from a particularly busy season of life. But that isn't necessarily fair to them or healthy for us! Here are a few ways to stay connected with the ones that you care about, even when you are busy . . .

Invite friends to run errands with you. You have to go to the grocery store or Target anyway, so why not invite a friend along? They probably have to go shopping at some point this week too so you can make it more enjoyable for both of you!

Send last-minute invites. It can be hard to know how your family is going to be feeling at any given moment—will they be tired, hungry, sick, or involved with extracurriculars? It feels daunting to commit to things well in advance, but how often do you find yourself with an hour or two of free time? Text those friends and invite them to the park or to the pizza place with you. Those spur-of-the-moment activities can be the most enjoyable!

Exercise with friends or family. Join the same gym, sign up for the same classes, or simply walk the same walking path together! The exercise itself will be more enjoyable, you will have an accountability partner, and you'll get to reconnect with your favorite people while keeping yourself healthy.

Text short messages. It can be sweet and meaningful to send your friends and family quick text messages or leave voicemails letting them know that you are thinking about them. It doesn't take a lot of time to send a thoughtful text, and it can be surprisingly refreshing to have some mini friend conversations built into the rest of your hectic week.

Keep a Regular Bedtime Routine
It can be hard to squeeze everything in and still get our kids (and ourselves) to bed at a reasonable hour. Of course, if we let bedtime fall to the back burner, we all suffer! Everyone is cranky, tired, and less productive than they need to be. Getting enough sleep is very important to managing your stress so here are a few ways to help keep bedtime more consistent . . .

Create a simple bedtime chart. This can help make the process go more smoothly for your kids (and for you)! It serves as a nice, visual reminder of the process; and helps to keep the routine consistent. (Visit AdoreThemParenting. com/Book-Resources for free printable bedtime charts.)

Keep track of the time. When life gets busy, it can be hard to do this simple task! Before you know it, it is already past ideal bedtimes, and you haven't even started the process. To help keep track of time, set an alarm on your phone so that it goes off at the same time each night telling you to start bedtime routines. You want this alarm to be for the beginning of the bedtime routine—not the time when you are hoping your kids are asleep.

Set aside time for quiet bonding activities. Trying to rush bedtime never works. Instead the kids fight it, and everyone ends up frustrated and awake instead of calm and asleep. It is worth scheduling an extra fifteen minutes into the bedtime routine to give your kids a chance to tell you stories, to ask them questions about their day, or to read an extra book together. Quiet together-time can work wonders at bedtime!

Make Time for Exercise

Making the most of your time is often about multitasking. How can I accomplish two important things at the same time? How can I make this fun and enjoyable instead of just feeling like another chore or task to check off the to-do list? Keep in mind that physical activity can be a great stress management tool, which means that we shouldn't stop exercising as our stress levels rise. Here are some tips for making exercise still happen when life gets busy . . .

Some exercise is better than no exercise. This is a hard principle for me to follow because it is ingrained in me that a workout should be an all-out sweaty activity. But I am slowly changing that mindset since I know there are benefits with even mild forms of exercise. Walking for twenty minutes can still be beneficial, and you are much more likely to follow through with something regularly if it doesn't feel so daunting.

Invite your friends to exercise with you. We mentioned this one above, but it's worth mentioning again! You can walk or jog much further while you are too busy chatting to notice how long you've been at it.

Find free workout videos. There are so many different exercise videos available for free online. You can tune in to anything from yoga to hip hop videos so that there is something for everyone. There are even videos geared toward kids that get the whole family moving.

Have fun playing a sport. This is another great way to incorporate exercise combined with family fun. Take your kids out to play soccer, tennis, basketball, or volleyball together. As long as you are all running around and having fun together, you can call it a success!

After reading through all of this, does it make you appreciate how much you expect yourself to do on a regular basis? We take on *a lot* as parents, and it is not surprising that we struggle with feeling overwhelmed and stressed out. So while we can use tips and strategies to help streamline, organize, and manage everything, we also need to keep tabs on our stress management and how much we are actually expecting of ourselves. We need to always be conscious of what a true work-life balance actually looks like, and then figure out how to get there!

*

Connect with Your Kids: Prepare for School

Back-to-school is always a weird time of year for families. Everyone is experiencing varying levels of dread, excitement, or both! Aside from the transition in seasons and schedules, we also have to address the questions of what might be best for our kids and our families as a whole each year. We are lucky to have a variety of education options available to us, but that doesn't necessarily make the decision any easier. There are pros and cons to any situation, and we can take some comfort in knowing that if something isn't working, we can always change course. When trying to figure out a school year plan for your kids, you have a lot to consider. Here are a few areas to think through in order to make your decision.

Consider Your Options

Something that has helped me a lot in all areas of my life is allowing myself to look at all of the options—not only the ones that I think will be the right fit for me. So when you are considering different education options, don't write off any of the methods even if you are pretty sure you don't want to go that route. Why? Because it will help you highlight the benefits of the other options on the table.

For example, I was talking with a mom who did not consider public school to be an option for her kids. She was looking at either homeschooling them or sending them to a small private school. When I asked her to picture what public school would look like, she was quick to say that that wasn't her preference, and they wouldn't be going in that direction. But I asked her to at least consider it as a part of a mental exercise. If your kids went to public school, you wouldn't have the burden of private school tuition. If your kids went to public school, you would have dedicated time during the day to focus on your work. While there are many other positive reasons to send your kids to public school, we were looking at the financial impact in this scenario. Public school would help bring some financial stability to the family. It was important to make note of this so that she would understand what she was sacrificing if she went a different route. They ended up being sacrifices that this mom was willing to make, but it helped her appreciate that they were doing a hard thing for the right reasons for their particular family.

On the other hand, there are many families who don't even want to consider the possibility of homeschooling. It feels like too much work, and they get overwhelmed at not even knowing where to start. No one is saying that you have to homeschool your kids, but you should at least keep the option on the table to be able to weigh the other options more accurately. If your child is struggling in school on an emotional or academic level, then it may be time to at least entertain other education options. Looking at alternative options may end up helping you troubleshoot struggles within the classroom.

Once you look outside the window of what you've always done, you will see that there are many other valid options out there. Speak with families pursuing these different options and begin to learn what has worked well for them and why. It is always surprising to see how much traditional education can vary from area to area. Something that is totally the norm in one school district may seem groundbreaking in another. Every kid's needs are a little different so it's okay to question the education options in front of you and weigh the alternatives.

Smooth Out the Logistics

It's not glamorous or warm and fuzzy, but figuring out the logistics of family life factors into educational decisions. Working from home may provide you with some flexibility, but not always. Before your kids head back to school (whatever that looks like), plan ahead, and make sure that the whole family is on the same page. Your kids will find comfort in knowing what their days will look like, and it encourages you to start brainstorming solid routines ahead of time.

This is also your chance to optimize your own schedule. I love that I can take a more laid-back approach to summer break, but I am always itching to dive back into more structure once school starts up again. You can't expect an entire family's worth of schedules to fall into place on their own so it's up to you to look at everything and start solving the time-management puzzle.

It can also be really helpful to minimize the extracurriculars in the fall as everyone adjusts to their school schedules. Early mornings and long days of learning can make for some very tired kids, so you don't want to add in any extras until you're sure that your child (and you) are up for it. I have seen the longing look in a fellow parent's eye when they ask about evening activities and I report back that we don't have anything going on. And while I see the value in extracurriculars throughout the year, I try to maintain a reasonable balance to maintain our sanity as a family.

Address Any Worries

Too often, kids worry to themselves in silence without bringing their concerns to their parents. It's our job as parents to check in with them and encourage them to express things that they might be worrying about or have questions about. There are many unknowns when heading into a new school year (especially if you are trying out a new method of learning), but many of those questions and worries have answers and solutions!

It's a good idea to involve your child in coming up with solutions for their concerns. If they are worried about new classmates, you can brainstorm some fun stories and conversation starters that they could use to connect with new friends. Never underestimate the power of a good script! If they are worried about their teacher, you could write an email together that introduces your child and asks the teacher about their three favorite things.

This will make the teacher feel friendly and familiar to your child. If your child is stressing about getting lost in a new building, request a map from the school and assure them that there will be other kids in the same situation. Taking that extra time to talk through these concerns before school starts will save you time and energy when it's actually time to head back to learning.

And while many of your child's concerns may seem small and trivial, it does not feel that way to them! It is crucial to give appropriate weight to their worries and help them get through things in a positive way. You are teaching them how to problem-solve, you are teaching them coping skills, and you are showing them that you'll always be there to support them.

Highlight the Positives

As adults, it can be tough to go back to work after a week of vacation so imagine what it's like for kids after having the whole summer off! They don't want to go back to their "jobs," which is exactly why it's important to highlight some of the positives of school. We can remind our children that school isn't all bad by asking questions like:

- Which friends are you excited to see?
- What art projects do you think you'll get to do this year?
- What is something that you really want to learn?

It always amazes me to see how much our children learn throughout the course of a school year, and it can be fun for them to reflect on just how far they've come. They can see that they are making progress even when the day-to-day feels monotonous. Look back through their old schoolwork from previous years and praise them for working so hard. Show them that their work pays off, and that things that were difficult for them a year ago, now seem easy.

We can also show our children the real world applications of their education. Why do they need to learn to read and write well? How can learning a math concept (even one that you may never use in the real world) help you work through other difficult problems that you may come across? While one subject may seem boring to learn about, you may discover a new subject that sparks a new passion in you. Some kids might be bored to tears learning about weather patterns and the names of the clouds, while others begin dreaming about being a meteorologist!

Partway through the summer, we start getting bombarded with back-to-school ads. Store shelves switch from beach towels and sand toys to backpacks and pencils super early, which can be a real downer for kids (and parents). Despite all of the buzz, it's important to be realistic about the time that you do have left in the summer. And your kids will appreciate you acknowledging that, sharing it with them, and helping them make the most of it!

Try to plan some fun activities and adventures toward the end of the summer break. Check off a few more of those summer bucket list items. And find a few ways to relax and recharge so that you can start the school year in the best way possible. Summer's not over quite yet, so make the most of it while you can!

*

Work from Home: Enjoy Your Work Day

We've been talking a lot about the difficulties of working from home, but we can't forget about the benefits! Working from home allows you a lot of flexibility that you wouldn't have otherwise, but you have to make sure that you are taking advantage of that freedom. I know firsthand how difficult that can be when you are in the midst of a hectic work week. I have found myself wishing for a dark cubicle with a door that closes to the outside world when I am frantically working on a big project. But when I remind myself that I can think outside the box, and do things to make my work day more enjoyable, everything starts to flow better.

Get Comfy

When I used to work in an office, one of my friends and coworkers had a comfy chair and blanket in the corner of her office. I loved walking through the door and seeing her snuggled up, looking cozy, and being productive. It was a reminder that we don't have to take ourselves so seriously—why not answer emails and take phone calls from a comfy corner? Since I do most of my work on my laptop, I tend to carry it around the house with me.

Sometimes I'm at my desk, but you can also find me typing away happily from my couch, my kitchen table, or even my bed.

I also joke that I will only do work that allows me to wear sweatpants—writing, running a website, being a mom, and even my past experience as a coach. My work-from-home wardrobe entails looking put-together on top—a nice shirt, makeup, and maybe even a necklace—with comfortable yoga pants on that I can swap out quickly for jeans or dress pants as needed.

Enjoy Music

Music has an incredible effect on our moods. And now that we have smartphones and smart devices, we are able to enjoy music in every room of the house! I have different songs that I put on when I need to tackle different tasks. I need to listen to instrumental music while I am writing because anything with words interrupts my thought process, but then I love to rock out to something more upbeat when I'm working on designing graphics or working through monotonous tasks.

Creating playlists for different tasks can also be a fun way to help your family go through their routines. My kids and I have a morning playlist that we listen and dance to on our way to the bus stop each morning. It wakes us up, gets us moving, and starts the day with some positive energy! You can use music to give your little athlete an extra boost of energy before their soccer game. You can share some of your own personal favorites during a fun dance party to unwind. And you can create a soothing playlist to help everyone calm down and relax before bedtime. Find some family favorites, put together a few playlists, and get creative with how you incorporate music into your family's routines.

Take Mental Breaks

One of the most frustrating things about watching a toddler fight taking a nap is knowing how badly you wish you could take a nap yourself. Naps aren't always a possibility for parents, but we can and should carve out time for a mental break in the afternoon. You don't necessarily need to fall asleep, but a few minutes away from your workload will help to reset your mind and reenergize your body. A mental break means that you turn off your brain as much as possible, even for a few minutes—lay down, close your eyes, and rest. The goal is to truly relax for a few moments. One of the best parts about working from home is that you can make this a daily ritual since our bodies naturally slow down in the afternoons anyway.

Note: Of course, we need to be aware of everyone's safety. If you are responsible for little kids, you have to be very careful of how much you tune out! This might only be possible during nap time if you have young kids. But we trust you will use your best judgment!

Remember to Eat

I always have good intentions of meal planning and preparing yummy, healthy meals for me and my family, but I have finally accepted that this is not one of my strengths. Instead, I try to stock up on breakfast and lunch options that are easy to grab and eat with little fuss and minimal mess. My work-from-home lunches usually consist of what I fondly call Adult Lunchables—some meat, some cheese, some crackers. And when I know I will have a particularly crazy work day, I pack lunches for me and the kids in the morning while I'm making breakfast so that when noon rolls around, we can simply grab them out of the refrigerator. Keeping it simple allows me to eat nourishing foods that keep me going throughout each workday.

Play with Your Kids

Our kids are the best built-in distraction! No matter how hard we try, they won't let us forget the importance of having fun. When you have a few moments when you can step away from your work, take that time to plug in to your kids. You can run around and play a quick game of tag, sit on the floor with them to build a new LEGO house, or ask them to tell you a silly story while you all snuggle on the couch. All of these little moments will help take your mind off of work, help you relax for a bit, and restore your energy and creativity for the rest of your work day. When we are purposeful about what we do with these short breaks, we can begin to feel more fulfilled and less guilty.

Go Outside

Working from home gives you the opportunity to go outside much more often than working in a typical office environment. You can take your work outside and enjoy some much-needed sunshine, you can go for a short walk around the neighborhood to reset your brain, or you can simply sit near a window to enjoy the natural light. Take the extra few minutes to set up a nice workstation outside for a literal change in scenery. And it is extra helpful when you can set things up in a way that you can get work done while watching your kids play outside.

Get Creative

As an adult, there is very little focus on creativity unless you happen to work in a creative field. But exploring creative outlets is a great way to renew your energy levels and unwind from a long day. Turn on some background music, gather the kids, put out a few bowls of your favorite snacks, and do something simple and creative together. I like to choose things that don't require a lot of preparation or brain power like doing a puzzle or coloring. Other times, I'll sit at the kitchen table and work on something by myself while my kids play nearby. Whether it's journaling, crocheting, or drawing, seeing something come together from the work of your own hands is very gratifying.

And don't get stuck in the trap of feeling like you have to make something beautiful enough to post on social media; that's not the point! The end goal is to simply enjoy doing an activity that exercises the creative part of your brain.

Reward Yourself

Just like you reward your kids for a job well done, set up rewards for yourself! Have something to look forward to at the end of each work day or after completing certain projects or tasks. Maybe there's a movie that you've been wanting to watch, or a book you've been excited to read. Maybe you are craving a high intensity workout class, or a night out with a friend. Even simple pleasures like a glass of your favorite drink on the back porch can feel rewarding.

The bottom line is this . . . don't get so bogged down in the details of each day that you forget to appreciate what you have. There are small things that you can do throughout your work days to make everything feel lighter. And once you feel refreshed, you will be better able to handle all of the responsibilities thrown your way!

*

Monthly Reflections

Since parenting requires so much from us day after day, it can be hard to slow down and take the time to reflect on what's working and what we need to change. You might be tempted to breeze past these monthly checkpoints, but we highly recommend that you take a few minutes to stop and reflect on the past month while it's still fresh in your mind.

There are a few reasons to do this exercise each month. First of all, it encourages you to live and parent more mindfully. It is a checkpoint so that you don't continue on the same path month after month, year after year. If something isn't working well for you and your family, you have the opportunity to identify that and begin to correct it!

It also gives you the opportunity to highlight and appreciate the things that *are* going well. Feeling gratitude for amazing people and moments in your life will lead to even more positivity in the following month. We want to train our brains to see the bright side, and monthly reflections are a simple way to do that.

Once you work through your monthly reflections, you may want to share your thoughts with trusted loved ones in your life. It is a great way to share insight with your partner, your coworkers, and your friends. You can share new ideas with them, and they will be able to support you moving forward as well!

August
Monthly Reflections

Five Highlights
What were your favorite moments from the month?

_____

_____

_____

Four Things You Focused on
What took up the most brain power this month?

_____

_____

_____

Three Game Changers
What were those a-ha moments?

_____

_____

_____

Two Things You Didn't Get to
Do you need to get to them next month?

_____

_____

_____

One Disappointment

Did you take time to grieve that moment?

_____

_____

_____

Next Month

What do you want to continue for the next month?

_____

_____

_____

What do you want to change for the next month?

_____

_____

_____

Notes

_____

_____

_____

_____

_____

_____

_____

_____

Chapter 9
September

With the family getting back into their normal school year routines, you may see some new areas of concern pop up. In this chapter, we encourage you to focus on your health and seek help when you need it. We also provide strategies for you to effectively advocate for your children's education. And we offer time-management tips to help you create fluid routines rather than rigid schedules.

*

Monthly Intentions
At the beginning of each month, we'll leave space for you to prioritize, plan, and prepare. As parents, our lives can start to feel like a series of small emergencies. One simple way to keep things organized is to set clear priorities and plan accordingly for the month ahead. Answering these five questions at the start of each month only takes a few minutes, but it will help you feel organized and ready to tackle the next thirty days.

Note: Daily and weekly plans are a great way to make sure that you are maintaining your monthly priorities and staying focused. Free printable planners can also be found on our website: AdoreThemParenting.com/Book-Resources.

September
Monthly Intentions

1. What are some things that I can do to improve my own well-being?

   _____

   _____

   _____

2. How can I support and connect with my partner?

   _____

   _____

   _____

3. What do my kids need me to make a priority?

   _____

   _____

   _____

4. What will I need to focus on for work?

   _____

   _____

   _____

5. Which household tasks or projects need my attention?

   _____

   _____

   _____

*

Focus on You: Focus on Your Health

Since we have so many responsibilities as parents, it's important that we are happy and healthy. We need to be able to provide a solid foundation for our families and the communities around us. And we can't do that if our own needs are not being met first.

The difficult part of having so many people rely on you is that there is very little time for yourself. As parents, we are used to rolling with the punches. We learn fairly quickly that our lives are at the mercy of our children—their activities, their moods, their health. We take them to the doctor when they catch the latest illness. But when we catch the same thing, we somehow keep functioning.

We love caring for our families, but in order to do so, we also need to care and advocate for ourselves! When it comes to my kids, my mama bear has been known to come out from time to time. I will fight for them to the ends of the earth, and I will make sure that I speak up for them even when it's extremely uncomfortable for me to do so. But when it comes to advocating for myself, I don't take that same approach. When it comes to me and my own health, my own needs, or my own wants, I don't fight quite as hard.

Maybe it's because we are already so exhausted. Maybe it's because it seems easier to walk away. Maybe it's because we think that if we ignore the problem long enough, it'll get better on its own. Maybe we are still secretly hoping that our own moms will waltz in and be our mama bears again.

But whatever the reason, we are not advocating for ourselves often enough. And I see it time and time again with parents in my own community. I see people suffering and struggling and not getting the treatment or recognition that they deserve. I see this most often when it comes to health concerns. How many of us parents are guilty of ignoring health problems for longer than we should? Me. And almost every other parent that I know.

Many people are suffering from chronic conditions that are going untreated. We think to ourselves, *Well, this is my new normal. I just need to cope with it.* However, this mentality is harmful to ourselves *and* our families. As parents, we need to begin taking our health seriously, and we need to encourage others to do the same.

Acknowledge You Need a Solution

First of all, let me assure you that I totally understand the hesitation here . . . no one wants to go digging for answers. It can be a long, difficult, and oftentimes expensive process. I have personally faced doctors who have dismissed my very real symptoms after running a few basic tests. I have been face-to-face with specialists who interrupted me mid-sentence when I was trying to convey important information about my medical history. But I have also seen the upside for advocating for myself and finding solutions to my medical concerns.

Most medical issues don't magically resolve on their own. In fact, most of them gradually worsen when not taken care of and treated properly. Even if you are still functioning, you probably have no idea how much this chronic issue is dragging you down. It can affect your moods, your overall health, and your relationships. Wondering if you are going to have a good day or a bad day is no way to live your life. You need to work toward finding a solution, being your own advocate, and finding a support system to help you through the process.

And I want to clarify that when I mention "chronic issue" I don't only mean huge scary medical issues like cancer. There are far too many parents living their lives suffering from chronic migraines, back pain, dietary intolerances, and other common concerns that are affecting their lives in a very real way. We shouldn't have to suffer on a daily basis. Fighting for a solution is worthwhile if it means that we can get to a happier and healthier place.

Find a Medical Professional

One of the most important steps is finding a medical professional that will truly work alongside you. Someone who will listen to you, is in it for the long haul, and is determined to figure out this puzzle one way or another.

When I was dealing with a difficult medical issue myself, I finally found a doctor who responded to my long list of symptoms by saying, "That is not normal. You should not have to live like that. We are going to get you feeling better." I cried on the spot because I was so relieved to have someone in my corner who was ready to partner with me to create a plan of action.

That doctor saw me as an individual human being who was going through something that negatively impacted my daily life. She didn't have the answer right then and there, but I didn't need her to have the answer right away. I just needed her to see me and acknowledge what I was going through. Over the course of the next year or so, we found the right solution for me. And years later, I have a whole new quality of life thanks to that process and the solutions that we found!

Keep Them Updated

What I discovered through that process of working with those incredible doctors who were willing to partner with me was that I still needed to be a big part of the equation. Whether you see your family doctor or a specialist, they can't read your mind. It is your responsibility to report back about what is working and what isn't since they are not typically making those kinds of follow-up calls if you do not initiate them. I learned this the hard way.

I gave one particular treatment six months to work because the Internet said that it could take up to six months for you to see results. It didn't work. I suffered through those six months, and then I reported that back to my doctor. She asked me why I waited so long to get back in touch with her if it wasn't working? And then she encouraged me to always follow up and give them updates about my health. She said that they assume that if they don't hear from a patient, they are doing well. Talk about a wake-up call!

Another important note about communicating with your medical professionals is that you never know which symptoms might be important. There might be something that seems unrelated to you that might spark a new idea for your doctor. It is important to track and communicate all of your symptoms clearly so that your doctor can have as much information as possible.

Allow Time to Seek Help and Heal

Getting and staying healthy takes time. It takes trial and error. It requires a lot of phone calls and appointments. It might also mean that you feel worse before you feel better. It will be frustrating so give yourself some extra grace during this time.

If you are dealing with a nagging health issue, you may need to reframe your thinking and make that your priority for a while. Try to cut back on extra projects or activities, reduce as many stressors as you can, and allow yourself to focus on your health. Be sure to reach out for help from others during this time as well! I am sure that your kids won't mind some extra playdates for a while.

The goal is to tackle this issue with your time and energy full-force so that you can move on and put it behind you. Maybe that means that you take a break from signing your kids up from activities for a season, or you back down from volunteer responsibilities for a bit. But if it means that you can jump back into all of that later on with a renewed sense of energy and with you in better health, it is absolutely worth it!

Addressing these health concerns head-on can be difficult, but it can also be hugely rewarding. Keep searching for those solutions. Keep working toward a healthier you because your family needs you at your best, and you deserve nothing less!

*

Connect with Your Kids: Advocate for Education

Education is one of the most important parts of childhood. Our kids deserve access to a great education and any extra support that they may need. Throughout our society, we are beginning to do a better job of understanding that everyone learns a little bit differently. There are different styles of learning that work for different people, and from an early age, students tend to gravitate to certain subjects.

Despite these shifts, there may still be times when you need to speak up and advocate for your child. This does not mean storming into the principal's office or complaining incessantly about your child's teacher. It means understanding your child's rights as a student, your important role as their parent, and how to build a team that will help them reach their potential.

Know Your Rights

As a parent, you hold the power. It might not always feel that way, but when it comes to advocating for your kid, you can make things happen. If you want full control of your child's education, then you may need to look into alternative learning methods such as homeschooling. But if they are struggling in a certain area, don't pull them out of that environment prematurely. You may have to accept some give-and-take, but oftentimes you can find a way to give your child a great school experience!

Start by going to your local Department of Education website. You might have to do some digging, and you will have to set aside some time for this research, but there are many helpful resources available to you online. The benefit of reading through actual government guidelines (instead of parenting forums) is that you will be able to identify your rights as a parent and your child's rights as a student. Knowing these rights can be extremely helpful when going into difficult advocacy situations where the school is giving you a hard time. And it is empowering to know that you've done your research and have the base knowledge to advocate for your child.

Reading through these documents always reminds me that education is extremely important and is a very serious issue. If your child is struggling, you don't have to watch it happen. You can take action! There are solutions.

Involve Your Student

It is very helpful to get feedback from your child as you work through this process. My child filled out a survey for one of his support teachers at the end of the school year, and on the form, he said that math was his least favorite subject. I was horrified. Math has always been his superpower, and

Student Survey

Print copies of this student survey at AdoreThemParenting.com/Book-Resources.

- What is your favorite subject?
- What is your least favorite subject?
- What is something that you'd like to learn more about?
- What is something that you are having trouble understanding?
- What do you want to be when you grow up?
- What is the best part about your school?
- What is something that you want your teachers to know about you?
- Is there someone at school that has been really helpful to you? Who was it, and how did they help?
- What is something that you would change about school if you could?
- Is there anything else that you want to share?

to find out at the end of the year that he wasn't enjoying it was a punch in the gut. What we found out was that he had been bored all year long, and he wasn't being challenged in that subject. From that point on, I vowed to check in with my child more often and not wait until the end of the school year to find out that something wasn't working.

Get Support

One of the first steps in receiving educational support for your child is requesting evaluations and assessments to better determine your child's strengths and struggles. Many parents avoid this step because they, understandably, want to steer clear of any possible stigma. It can be difficult to have your child receive a diagnosis, and you certainly don't want a label to be detrimental to them. However, I try to think about this concern in a different way. If the signs and symptoms are there, does it really matter what we call it? The labels that get assigned to these behaviors and struggles are simply a pathway to much-needed resources. My child won't be able to receive speech therapy unless they first identify a speech and language deficit. My child will have access to additional and focused resources after uncovering that they struggle with dyslexia. A diagnosis of autism may be difficult to process, but it opens the doors to resources and therapies that can be incredibly helpful. The point is that regardless of what we call it, your child's strengths and struggles will be there. It's not a perfect system, but sometimes the gateway to support is a diagnosis.

Communicate Effectively

Arguably the most important part of advocating for our children is communicating with the rest of the team. Your child's team may consist of teachers, administrators, therapists, doctors, and of course, caregivers. There can be a lot of people involved that all have different areas of expertise, different insights, and different opinions based on their interactions with your child. While you are the expert on your kid, the rest of the team has a lot of valuable insight to offer as well.

Trust me, I get it. When your child is struggling with something, it's hard not to march into the school office and start demanding that things need to change. However, I have found that a lighter approach is often more effective. If you want to be taken seriously, if you want the other members of the team to truly listen to you, you have to cool down, collect your thoughts, and approach the situation strategically.

Take the time to figure out what you want to accomplish. What do you think your child needs, and how do you think the team can help fulfill that need? Sometimes you might simply feel like you need more information, and then you can bring that to the people who have more resources at their disposal. They are not the enemy, and this is likely not the first time they have seen this situation. Keeping them updated and giving them insight into how your child is doing outside of the school environment can be critical information to help the rest of the team see the full picture.

Teachers are often very open to suggestions when you take a calm approach. I am always very sympathetic to how much teachers have to manage on a regular basis, and I am not there to make their job harder. But sometimes, I may have a simple solution to help my child and the teacher. For example, my child always forgot to turn in his homework in a certain class. The teacher had emailed me letting me know that this was a problem, and I felt like I had a simple solution. I asked her to write, "Turn in homework," on a sticky note and place it on the corner of his desk. It was quick, easy, and effective! The teacher didn't have to keep reminding my child, and he learned some independence and a life skill—we all need written reminders sometimes.

Overall, you have to keep in mind that your student is not the only student. Every part of the team cares about your child and wants to be able to provide them with the best experience possible. But . . . like you, they have other responsibilities. We can advocate for our children while also being reasonable with what we are asking the team to do. How can we work within the constraints of an imperfect system to help our kids thrive?

*

Work from Home: Establish Realistic Routines

When working from home, it can be more helpful to think about creating a routine rather than a schedule. A schedule is often too rigid for everyday family life. Kids cover themselves in peanut butter, spouses have car trouble, and computers crash. Hopefully all of these things don't happen on the same day, but as you know all too well, I can't make any promises!

Creating a routine allows each day to have a familiar flow without the pressures of a strict schedule. And while I'd love to give you some sample routines to start implementing in your own home, I know how different each situation can look. Your routine will have to be customized to you, your work, and your family. Working from home with toddlers looks very different from working from home with preteens. Having a flexible work schedule means that your routines can vary more than someone who has to be clocked in during certain hours throughout the day. Despite these variables, there are a few things that you can consider to create helpful routines for your household.

Be Flexible

A common issue that I see work-from-home parents facing is that they want to have set times for set tasks. Sure, some jobs will require you to have set hours and rigid schedules, but for the most part, employers are happy as long as you are still getting things done in a timely manner. If your daily schedule is planned down to the minute, you are in for a rough day. It takes time and energy to do all of that planning, and it is extremely frustrating when things don't end up going according to plan—which they never do—because you have kids.

Your day might include a few important appointments, calls, or meetings. You have to show up on time for doctor appointments, virtual meetings, and soccer practice; but aside from that, it is helpful to practice being more flexible. This concept works in two ways—both when things are going well and when they're not. If you are feeling inspired, run with it! I have been caught in the trap of thinking that I have all the time in the world to get a project done so then I let inspiration pass me by. The "I'll do it later" mentality can turn into a real problem—especially while raising a family. Suddenly I find myself under a tight deadline when I should have gotten it over with when I was feeling motivated.

The same rules of flexibility apply for when you (or your kids) are having a really rough time. There will be grouchy days. It's a rule of life. There will be days when everyone is a little tired, a little under the weather, and you wish you could crawl back into bed. So do it (if you can), but not for the whole day. It's okay to crawl back into bed and rest your eyes for a few minutes after your child woke up three times during the night. If you take those moments to relax, you have a better chance of being productive throughout the rest of the day. When you try to power through those tough moments, you end up staring blankly at your computer screen or making mistakes that you'll have to fix later. Walk away, restore a bit of your energy, and come back to it later.

Tune into You

From the time we were young children ourselves, we were pushed into a schedule that was accepted by society as a whole. You woke up at a certain time, made it to school at a certain time, ate dinner at a certain time, went to activities at a certain time, and tried to go to bed at a certain time to be able to do it all again the next day. Despite a lifetime of that rhythm, my body never felt like it adjusted. I hate mornings. And I can't tell you how grateful I am to be able to work from home and set my own hours so that I can capitalize on when I'm naturally most alert and productive.

You may not have complete control over your schedule, but working from home often gives you more options for your day than working at an office. Start keeping track of your workflow. When you seem to fly through a certain task with ease, what time is it? When you find yourself staring at your work unable to make sense of it, what time is it? Once you start figuring out your natural rhythms, you will be able to make them work in your favor!

It is common for people's brains to work really well mid-morning, which can be a great time for analytical tasks that require a lot of brainpower. Afternoons are a wash for most people. It is a natural slump, and you aren't the only one that feels like their afternoon would be better spent taking a nap. And then there is some magic in the evenings when your brain has been working hard all day long but gets a second wind. It can be the perfect time for creative work because you aren't overanalyzing everything you're doing, yet you still have enough brainpower left to let things flow naturally.

Of course, this isn't the case for every individual. And, of course, you have many other demands placed on you throughout each and every day. We aren't functioning in a bubble by ourselves where we can follow our body's every cue, but we can pay attention and try to give ourselves every advantage that we can.

And on a final note, keep in mind that these routines might need to change from week to week. Something that worked well for the last few months may suddenly stop working for everyone as you enter a new stage of family life. As we discuss throughout this book, the best we can do is try something, see how it goes, and change course as needed!

*

Monthly Reflections

Since parenting requires so much from us day after day, it can be hard to slow down and take the time to reflect on what's working and what we need to change. You might be tempted to breeze past these monthly checkpoints, but we highly recommend that you take a few minutes to stop and reflect on the past month while it's still fresh in your mind.

There are a few reasons to do this exercise each month. First of all, it encourages you to live and parent more mindfully. It is a checkpoint so that you don't continue on the same path month after month, year after year. If something isn't working well for you and your family, you have the opportunity to identify that and begin to correct it!

It also gives you the opportunity to highlight and appreciate the things that *are* going well. Feeling gratitude for amazing people and moments in your life will lead to even more positivity in the following month. We want to train our brains to see the bright side, and monthly reflections are a simple way to do that.

Once you work through your monthly reflections, you may want to share your thoughts with trusted loved ones in your life. It is a great way to share insight with your partner, your coworkers, and your friends. You can share new ideas with them, and they will be able to support you moving forward as well!

September
Monthly Reflections

Five Highlights
What were your favorite moments from the month?

_____

_____

_____

Four Things You Focused on
What took up the most brain power this month?

_____

_____

_____

Three Game Changers
What were those a-ha moments?

_____

_____

_____

Two Things You Didn't Get to
Do you need to get to them next month?

_____

_____

_____

One Disappointment

Did you take time to grieve that moment?

_____

_____

_____

Next Month

What do you want to continue for the next month?

_____

_____

_____

What do you want to change for the next month?

_____

_____

_____

Notes

_____

_____

_____

_____

_____

_____

_____

_____

_____

Chapter 10
October

This month offers opportunities for your family to keep working toward individual goals and reconnect through quality time. This chapter provides inspiration to turn your home into a peaceful retreat with budget-friendly tips. We share fun fall activities for families to connect with each other and make the most of the season. And we cover ways that you can build your network to establish a sense of community and support while working from home.

*

Monthly Intentions

At the beginning of each month, we'll leave space for you to prioritize, plan, and prepare. As parents, our lives can start to feel like a series of small emergencies. One simple way to keep things organized is to set clear priorities and plan accordingly for the month ahead. Answering these five questions at the start of each month only takes a few minutes, but it will help you feel organized and ready to tackle the next thirty days.

Note: Daily and weekly plans are a great way to make sure that you are maintaining your monthly priorities and staying focused. Free printable planners can also be found on our website: AdoreThemParenting.com/Book-Resources.

October
Monthly Intentions

1. What are some things that I can do to improve my own well-being?

_____

_____

_____

2. How can I support and connect with my partner?

_____

_____

_____

3. What do my kids need me to make a priority?

_____

_____

_____

4. What will I need to focus on for work?

_____

_____

_____

5. Which household tasks or projects need my attention?

_____

_____

_____

*

Focus on You: Make Your Home a Retreat

Leaving town, getting away, and enjoying a relaxing retreat sounds pretty incredible, but it isn't always possible to arrange. And while these weekend getaways can be wonderful and restorative, you still need to return home at some point. Walking through your front door shouldn't instantly stress you out, which is why we are sharing concepts and strategies for making your house feel more like home.

It can be really difficult when the days get shorter. Who wants to leave the house and drive to an after-school activity when it's already dark out? I used to dread these dark winter days, and it would really affect my mood, energy levels, and productivity. But then I discovered *hygge*.

Hygge is a Danish word that most closely translates to "cozy" in English, but the concept goes deeper than that. The word is meant to convey the idea of celebrating a time of year where you slow down, snuggle in, and enjoy the comforts of home. Instead of feeling despair that it's cold and dark, you look forward to a simpler time when you can be content in your own home. Start a fire, light some candles, grab some soft blankets, put on some music, and appreciate time spent together with your family. *Hygge* is meant to convey a sense of well-being and appreciation for the simple comforts in life, and the word alone feels like it's wrapping you in a fleece blanket!

I fell in love with this word and all that it represents. Anytime that I start to feel down about the literal darkness outside, I consider how I can bring some *hygge* into my home. Warm drinks, hearty soups, and fluffy pastries all provide a good dose of yummy *hygge* from the kitchen. Thick socks, oversized sweatpants, and bulky sweaters represent the *hygge* wardrobe. It's about savoring comforts and appreciating a slower pace. When I think of this concept, I picture a friend, wrapped up in a blanket, smiling at me over a cup of tea. And there's something about that image that instantly puts me in a good mood!

So how can you use this concept of *hygge* and create small spaces that feel like a mini getaway right in your own home? Sure, the central areas of the house might always be a bit of a mess because they get the most use, but the goal is to carve out calming spaces that give you a chance to relax and recharge. The following areas of your home have great potential for being mini retreats in the midst of an otherwise busy household, and all of these changes can be made on a tight budget. Find ways to rearrange and repurpose items that you already have in your home or enjoy exploring secondhand stores for great bargains.

Bedroom

I have to admit that my bedroom often looks more like a laundry room than a restful retreat. But when I consistently make the effort to keep the bedroom clutter-free, it is such a great experience. The first step with any calming space is keeping it clean and simple. Try to come up with systems and routines that will allow you to keep the bedroom a bedroom instead of a multipurpose room. Rearrange furniture and see which configuration makes the most sense. New bedding doesn't have to be expensive to revive the space. Beautiful colors, soft fabrics, and comfortable pillows will make you feel spoiled every time you crawl under the covers. Continually clear off your nightstand so that it's both visually relaxing and functional. And choose a candle with a mild, relaxing scent. By taking these few simple steps, you will be able to transform your bedroom into a fresh, inviting space.

Bathroom

If you share a bathroom with your kids, I'm sorry . . . this one is going to be a little trickier to maintain. Trickier, but still doable! I grew up in a one-bathroom house, and we lived in a one-bathroom house for quite a few years as a young family ourselves so I understand the struggles of sinks filled with toothpaste and towels on the floor. While the upkeep might be a little more intense with a shared bathroom, the tips for creating a light, enjoyable space are the same. Purchase big, fluffy, white towels that remind you of the spa and keep the space looking brighter. Choose candles that match the space; my kids love the smell of cookie-scented candles, but the bathroom isn't really the place for them. Organize the bathroom so that it is very functional for your family's needs and make it as easy as possible for each toiletry item to be returned to its proper spot. Create a basket of your own favorite pampering items like face masks, lotion, and hair treatments so that you can treat yourself whenever you have a few spare moments. You can also set up a space outside of the bathroom in your bedroom or your closet where you can do your hair and makeup without needing to use the shared bathroom space.

Outdoor Space

Being outside, even for a few minutes, can be extremely restorative. And you don't need a large space in order to enjoy the fresh air. Think about the outdoor spaces around your house and choose a spot that you can turn into a mini retreat. You'll want an area that is low-maintenance and cozy. Whether it's a deck, patio, or front porch, you can get creative. The most important thing to remember is that this space has to weather the elements. An outdoor couch on the deck sounds like a great idea until you realize that you will need to move the cushions off and on to avoid the rain. Find seating that is both comfortable and weather resistant. Add a small, sturdy side table for drinks and books. Since the sun sets early in October, add some fun lighting to boost your mood and encourage you to utilize the space even once the sun goes down. The whole point of this space is to make it easy for you to grab a hot cup of coffee and a blanket, and go outside for a few minutes even in the dead of winter.

Reading Corner

You don't need a large library to enjoy the magic of reading. Simply carving out a small reading corner can be a cozy, enjoyable experience. If possible, choose an area near a window so that you can enjoy the benefits of soaking in natural light. Pick out a comfy chair that allows you to put your feet up, and keep a snuggly blanket draped over it at all times. Place a lamp beside the chair for evening reading and plug your phone in to charge on the other side of the room to minimize distractions. Curate a stack of books and magazines to keep right beside your chair in a cute box or on a nice bookshelf. It doesn't have to be anything fancy since the goal is to simply get lost in your book for a little while!

Creative Space

Speaking of losing ourselves, having a creative process that you love is such an important part of being able to recharge. Whether you love to scrapbook, paint, sew, doodle, write, make music, or any other creative outlet, you deserve to have a small, dedicated space for that creative process. Many of us are guilty of taking over the kitchen table and then getting frustrated when our families interrupt us. But even in small homes, it's worth trying to troubleshoot this issue. Is there a closet that could be repurposed? Do you use your formal dining room, or could it be a music room? Is there a corner of your bedroom that could be a quiet writing station? You want to find a space where you can spread out and have all of your supplies ready and waiting for inspiration to strike. Take the time to organize this space and make it as functional and comfortable as possible so that you will be able to truly enjoy the creative process.

While all of these ideas take some thought and planning, the payoff is worth it! You deserve to have spaces throughout your home that you truly love. And as you create these mini retreats throughout your home, make sure that you are decorating with colors and textures that appeal to you personally. Display those keepsakes and treasures that bring you joy so that you have spaces around each corner that make you smile.

*

Connect with Your Kids: Enjoy Fall Family Activities

This time of year brings with it many changes and exciting activities! When I lived up north, the air would turn crisp pretty quickly. While we had to rush to squeeze it all in, we loved dressing in jeans with flannel shirts and boots, as we sipped something warm. But now living in the south, the fall oftentimes provides some of the best beach weather! No matter where you live, there are many fun opportunities for you and your family to get outside and enjoy making memories together.

Below you'll find a list of ideas that you can use to start your own Family Fall Bucket List. You can type it up, print it out, and even frame it to enjoy year after year. Give the kids a dry-erase marker to check off each activity as you enjoy them. (Print out our Fall Family Bucket List at AdoreThemParenting.com/Book-Resources.)

Some of these items you may need to save up for or work into the family budget, but there are also a lot of options that are free or won't cost much at all. Whether you invite family and friends to join you, or spend time together with your own kids, these fall-themed activities are a great way to share some laughs, try new experiences, and create some fun lasting memories.

At Home

Our family tries to pack in as much summer fun as we can, which often means that we are ready for a slower pace throughout the fall season. As the sun starts setting earlier, you have the perfect excuse to snuggle up on the couch as a family. Root for your favorite football team, watch a spooky movie, or get out some old childhood classics. And get a few Halloween or fall-themed books from the library to read together. Or maybe you're feeling inspired to transform the house, so put on a Halloween playlist, light a fall-scented candle, and start crafting!

Decorate the Front Door: One of my kids' favorite things to do is make our front door look like a monster. It's a simple craft where you only need paper, tape, and a little inspiration to turn your front door into a goofy monster. Will it have one eye or five? Will it have sharp teeth or a stitched-up Frankenstein smile? Let your kids take the lead and see what they come up with!

Make a Q-Tip Skeleton: This is an easy craft to do with little kids, but even older children will have fun with it! Get a black marker and draw the head of a skeleton (or your child can draw one) on a white piece of paper. Cut out the head, and glue it to a black piece of paper. Grab a whole bunch of Q-tips and have your child glue them onto the black paper to create an entire skeleton body.

Fall Family Fun in the Kitchen

1. Drink apple cider
2. Bake pumpkin bread
3. Dip candy apples
4. Cook pumpkin pancakes
5. Make caramel corn
6. Roast pumpkin seeds
7. Create jack-o-lanterns
8. Sip pumpkin spice lattes
9. Roast marshmallows and make s'mores
10. Bake apple, pumpkin, or pecan pies

Create a Thankful Tree: Purchase a piece of poster board, and draw a large tree with branches on it. Have your kids cut out leaves of different shapes and colors. Talk about what you are all thankful for, and write those things on the leaves. Then glue the leaves to your Thankful Tree!

Out and About

It's probably not the best idea to sit at home and eat freshly baked apple pies every evening, so here are a few ideas that will get you and your family out of the house . . .

Fall Festivals and Fairs: In our area, there are a lot of town fairs that happen throughout the month. These fairs are often packed with families and are a great place to stroll around, grab some food, and hang out with friends.

Football Games: Attending a tailgate can be a lot of fun and a great fall experience. But even if you can't make it to a big game, consider heading over to a local high school. It's budget-friendly, you can support the local athletes, and your kids will get to experience it all on a smaller scale.

Boo Your Neighbors: What does it mean to "boo your neighbor?" It is a simple, fun, pass-it-forward type of game that the kids can get involved with. Put together a simple basket of treats, include a note explaining to the recipient that they've "Been Boo'd," and the trend will spread throughout the neighborhood.

Corn Mazes and Hay Rides: Bring some friends, split up into teams, and race to the end of the maze; or simply work together. There are usually varying levels of difficulty for families with kids of different ages. Hay rides are another fun option for the whole family especially if you have a tractor-obsessed toddler in the group!

Fall Photo Walk: Fall is the perfect time to take a photo walk as a family. Give your kids your smartphone, an iPad, or an old digital camera and let them walk around capturing the beautiful scenery. Be sure to print out and display a couple favorites when you're done. Fall is also a great time to update your family photos and get some good options for your holiday cards.

Haunted Houses and Ghost Tours: These are so not my thing, but I know there are many people that genuinely enjoy the rush of being scared. Check your local area and do your research to find an option that will be a good fit for your family. You don't want anyone to be too terrified after an evening of supposed fun!

Bike Riding and Hiking: It gets so hot over the summer that going for a bike ride or a hike isn't as enjoyable as it could be! Autumn is a great time to get out those bikes, put air in the tires, and find a nice trail close to where you live. Or if that feels like too much of a hassle, you should be able to find scenic hiking trails worthy of a day trip in your area.

While some of these activities will have to be adjusted depending on the ages of your kids, they should spark some inspiration. There is so much to enjoy this time of year! And if you have an older teenager in the house, these suggestions can also provide some fun experiences for them to try with their friends. Happy fall, y'all!

*

Work from Home: Build Your Network

Building your network can be tricky when you're working from home, but there are still great opportunities to establish a sense of community and support. It is important to have people around you that understand the strange struggles of working from home. This network can help with motivation, brainstorming, and encouragement while you work to progress in your career.

Join Local and Online Communities

Whatever you are interested in, dive in with both feet! There are endless online communities filled with people sharing helpful information and opportunities. You don't necessarily have to spend endless hours engaging in these groups. It's okay to watch and learn. I have found job opportunities, freelance gigs, speaking engagements, new contacts, and other helpful career opportunities through online groups.

There are also incredible opportunities to be found through local groups in your area. There are the more well-known business groups that can be found in each community, but there are also likely some groups that you have never heard of. After working from home for over a decade, I only recently started making it a point to go out and find these local communities. And what I found was a group of like-minded professionals doing amazing things! I began to find people that were able to introduce me to other resources, and I was able to do the same for them.

We cannot function in a bubble. The nature of any career is that it needs a support system to flourish. Keep putting yourself out there, and you never know what might come your way.

Win at Networking

When I hear the phrase "networking," I picture a room full of men in suits swapping business cards and reciting canned elevator pitches. But that doesn't have to be you. Networking can be hugely beneficial to your career, and there are ways to go about it in a way that feels more natural to you and the people around you.

At a networking event, it's more beneficial for you to listen and engage with the person that you are meeting, than to do all of the talking yourself. People are quick to open up once you show them that you are genuinely interested; and this allows you to learn more about this person, what they do, and how you might be able to help. When you're able to provide value to the person you're speaking with, you win at networking. You might be able to help that person directly, or you might provide value by referring them to someone else. Either way, your new contact will leave the conversation feeling glad that they took the time to talk with you.

Networking is not your time to close a deal or even make a new pitch. It's your chance to collect the contact information of anyone that you meet at these events. And then it is important to make the effort to follow up with those contacts. If you promised to send over some resources, or connect them with someone else, do that promptly. And if not, you can send them a nice message telling them that you enjoyed meeting them and hope to touch base again.

Always Be Professional

It's a small world. Which is a very cliché thing to say, but you know exactly what I mean. And despite the global reach of this digital era, the world somehow feels even smaller. You respond to a friend's social media post, but you have no idea who is actually reading your comment. You lash out at a school administrator out of frustration, only to find out that their spouse is the manager at the company you just applied for. You miss a deadline for a freelance project and lose the opportunity to work on their next, larger project.

Along with being professional, you always want to help others within your network. I make it a point to send my contacts interesting opportunities that I think might be a good fit for them. I am always happy to make a recommendation when someone asks. And I love connecting people that may not have known each other otherwise.

It can feel a bit daunting. And, of course, you don't have to be perfect all of the time. But what it really boils down to is this . . . be kind and professional—no matter who you think is watching.

Put Yourself Out There

I have had multiple opportunities in my life where friends have asked, "How did you get that?" My answer has always been, "I applied for it!" I don't have any friends in high places, and I don't have any secret methods. When I see a big opportunity, I apply for it. I don't talk myself out of it. Even if I think it's a long-shot, I let *them* tell me "no" instead of disqualifying myself.

One time a friend sent me the form to apply for a speaking engagement, and without much thought I jumped on the computer and filled out the application to the best of my ability. A few months later, I got the exciting email that I was selected to come speak at the event. That email also contained the information that Michelle Obama, Brené Brown, and Shonda Rhimes would be speaking at the event. I was over the moon and ended up having an incredible experience because I filled out a simple online application one afternoon.

However, for every amazing opportunity that has panned out, there have been countless things that never ended up going anywhere. But when you are consistently putting yourself out there, it doesn't sting as much when you inevitably get some rejections. Don't wait until the perfect opportunity comes along—take chances along the way so that you'll be better prepared when faced with the next step.

Invest Your Time Wisely

Not every opportunity is a good opportunity. There are plenty of things that seem to be the right move on paper, but they suck the life right out of you. There are also many reasons for accepting opportunities such as making connections, gaining experience, establishing credibility, earning money, or a combination of these things. It's important that we take the time to evaluate the big picture before making decisions. If you can picture your ideal end result, then you will be able to work backward to figure out how to get there.

Once you know what you want, you will be able to accept opportunities that feel purposeful instead of only being time-consuming. However, there isn't always a straight, clear path to attaining your goals. You never know who you might meet, and who they might be able to connect you with! I have established great connections through volunteering within our local community. Volunteering at school, sitting on committees, and simply attending community town halls are all opportunities to meet people in your local community, share your own thoughts, advocate for your values, and help make your area a better place for fellow families.

It is also extremely helpful to simply start doing what you want to do. We live in a world where we have so much opportunity at our fingertips. You can find endless videos, articles, and books that will help you learn new skills. Begin to treat your future goals as your hobby so that you can hone your craft without the expectation of making money. Invest your time and learn along the way, and things will start to fall into place. Every step requires hard work, perseverance, and consistency. And if you are putting in the work behind the scenes, keep taking the chances that could propel you forward toward your bigger goals!

*

Monthly Reflections

Since parenting requires so much from us day after day, it can be hard to slow down and take the time to reflect on what's working and what we need to change. You might be tempted to breeze past these monthly checkpoints, but we highly recommend that you take a few minutes to stop and reflect on the past month while it's still fresh in your mind.

There are a few reasons to do this exercise each month. First of all, it encourages you to live and parent more mindfully. It is a checkpoint so that you don't continue on the same path month after month, year after year. If something isn't working well for you and your family, you have the opportunity to identify that and begin to correct it!

It also gives you the opportunity to highlight and appreciate the things that *are* going well. Feeling gratitude for amazing people and moments in your life will lead to even more positivity in the following month. We want to train our brains to see the bright side, and monthly reflections are a simple way to do that.

Once you work through your monthly reflections, you may want to share your thoughts with trusted loved ones in your life. It is a great way to share insight with your partner, your coworkers, and your friends. You can share new ideas with them, and they will be able to support you moving forward as well!

October
Monthly Reflections

Five Highlights
What were your favorite moments from the month?

_____

_____

_____

Four Things You Focused on
What took up the most brain power this month?

_____

_____

_____

Three Game Changers
What were those a-ha moments?

_____

_____

_____

Two Things You Didn't Get to
Do you need to get to them next month?

_____

_____

_____

One Disappointment

Did you take time to grieve that moment?

_____

_____

_____

Next Month

What do you want to continue for the next month?

_____

_____

_____

What do you want to change for the next month?

_____

_____

_____

Notes

_____

_____

_____

_____

_____

_____

_____

Chapter 11
November

November kicks off the start of the holiday season, which is a busy time for families. This month, we focus on simple ways that you and your family can give back to your local community. We provide parenting strategies that will encourage your kids to play more independently. And we share tips for planning ahead and optimizing your schedule for the upcoming holidays.

*

Monthly Intentions
At the beginning of each month, we'll leave space for you to prioritize, plan, and prepare. As parents, our lives can start to feel like a series of small emergencies. One simple way to keep things organized is to set clear priorities and plan accordingly for the month ahead. Answering these five questions at the start of each month only takes a few minutes, but it will help you feel organized and ready to tackle the next thirty days.

Note: Daily and weekly plans are a great way to make sure that you are maintaining your monthly priorities and staying focused. Free printable planners can also be found on our website: AdoreThemParenting.com/Book-Resources.

November
Monthly Intentions

1. What are some things that I can do to improve my own well-being?

_____

_____

_____

2. How can I support and connect with my partner?

_____

_____

_____

3. What do my kids need me to make a priority?

_____

_____

_____

4. What will I need to focus on for work?

_____

_____

_____

5. Which household tasks or projects need my attention?

_____

_____

_____

*

Focus on You: Help Your Community

Part of what makes your house a home is the local community surrounding and supporting you. Having lived in various areas, we feel so lucky to have settled into a home where our neighbors also value a sense of closeness—it makes a world of difference when raising a young family! And while we can't always know the neighborhood before we move into a new home, we can always make strides to improve our own local communities.

I had a philosophy professor in college that spoke about the concept of "giving until it hurts." He made the point that we should give until it hurts with the key word being "until." We don't need to hurt ourselves by giving; we should always be charitable up until the point where it starts to "hurt." Sure, we can give beyond that point; but it was an important concept to understand that there is truly no reason for not being generous with our time or resources if it is not negatively impacting us in any way.

Taking that concept, there are many things that we can do within our local communities that allow us to give until it hurts. We can step up as leaders in our area and do small things that will encourage positive changes. As a family, we can take small actions that will help others in our town without overwhelming ourselves in the process.

In this section, you will find great ideas for how you can give back to others; and as always, you will need to figure out the right balance for your family. Giving back can provide a sense of fulfillment and purpose while distracting you from your own struggles. And sometimes this shift in perspective is exactly what we need. However, these ideas are meant to be inspiring, not to make you feel guilty. Do what you can in this current season of life, and then consistently reevaluate your capabilities as things change.

Connect People

Part of being helpful to the people in your community is connecting them. If you know people who you think would make great friends, introduce them to each other. Connect neighbors to local resources that they might need. Keep an ear out for job openings and pass them along to others who might be a good fit. If you aren't able to help someone yourself, try to connect them with a person or organization that can. And introduce yourself to fellow parents at the playground, library, community events, and school functions. Simply looking out for opportunities and connections is a great way to establish ties and goodwill throughout your town.

Support Seniors

The seniors within your community may or may not have a good support system currently, but you and your family can always bring some joy to them through simple acts of kindness. Visit your local senior centers, nursing homes, and retirement communities. You can ask them directly how you might be able to help, and even taking the time to sit and listen to their stories can be incredibly moving. Check in with elderly neighbors to see if they need help with groceries; you can either pick up groceries for them or help them set up delivery services. Take the time to help someone when you see them struggling at the store (I once spent fifteen minutes helping an elderly gentleman pick out a great hair spray for his wife, and he was the sweetest man). Have your kids color pictures and drop them off at the homes of senior citizens in your community to bring a smile to their faces.

Volunteer Your Time

While volunteering can be time-consuming, it is also a very valuable and worthwhile experience for all involved! There are so many incredible community organizations that fly under the radar. Make an effort to discover these groups and see how you might be able to help support them. What skills do you have that you can offer? Consistently writing a newsletter for them, offering free photography, and teaching computer skills can all be valuable to your local organizations that may not have the resources to hire outside help. Volunteering at your child's school is a great way to get to know the students and teachers within the building, and I know firsthand that kindergarten teachers are always grateful to have someone else cut one hundred colorful triangles instead of having to do it themselves! Become a mentor through a local youth organization to help support the next generation. Check in with your local hospital and see if they need greeters or other volunteers to help make the hospital a more pleasant place. There are endless ways to volunteer your time, and it will be so appreciated!

Small Acts of Kindness

If you are not feeling up for taking on any more responsibility, there are still ways that you can spread kindness throughout your community!

1. Pay for the order behind you in line at the drive-through.
2. Compliment fellow parents when you see them out and about doing a good job parenting their kids, or pass them a knowing smile when their kid is having a tantrum in the middle of the store.
3. Send a quick text of encouragement to a friend before a big interview, meeting, or presentation.
4. Be polite to everyone that you interact with throughout the day (even if they are being rude to you).
5. When asked if you'd like to donate to charity at the check-out counter, say "yes."
6. Compliment a coworker in front of others when they go above and beyond.
7. Add coins to a parking meter if you notice that it is about to run out.
8. Patiently help a friend work through a hard decision.
9. Take the time to actually fill out those customer service surveys and give them a rave review.
10. When someone has had a significant impact on your life, reach out to let them know.

Regardless of what you choose to do, these small gestures can make a big difference in the lives of others. These simple ways of helping others allow us to give back to our community, but they also help us be better role models for our kids. When our kids see us being kind and helpful to the people around us, they will begin to do the same.

*

Connect with Your Kids: Encourage Independent Play

Wouldn't it be nice if children could just play happily by themselves whenever we had something to work on? Unfortunately that doesn't always happen, but there are things that we can do to help encourage independent play. We can teach our kids how to play alone, or with their siblings without interrupting us every five minutes.

The first step in encouraging independent play is spending a little bit of time getting the kids all set up so that you can take a step back. Children can have a hard time starting something on their own, but we can help lead the way. Before you dive into a work or house project, take a few minutes to make sure that everyone has gone to the bathroom, has their sippy cup filled, and has had a recent snack. And then help them set up their toys in a way that will be fun and engaging for them. For some kids, all you have to do is get down on the floor, dump out a bucket of blocks, and start building quietly yourself. For others, you may need to get a little more creative to really grab their attention and help them get immersed in play.

Find Toys that Hold Their Attention

Try to find toys that will hold your child's attention for more than a few minutes. This often means getting out toys that provide open-ended play instead of the latest gadget marketed to kids. The other key to creating a setup that holds your child's attention is combining toys that don't necessarily come in the same set. For example, Lincoln Logs and construction trucks are both fun toys, but together they provide twice the fun! Place the Lincoln Logs on one side of the room, and explain to your kids that they'll need to haul them in their trucks to the build site on the other side of the room. Or create a village filled with all of their favorite characters—Imaginext, Shopkins, Hatchimals, Barbies, superheroes, My Little Pony, dinosaurs, etc. Your kids can build them homes out of LEGOs or use existing doll houses. Give each character their own silly vehicle to drive around in, and then let the kids have fun with some great imaginative play. Look around the house, and see if you can find new combinations of toys to jump-start some creative play!

Rotating toys can also be a great way to keep your kids occupied. Of course kids want to play with their new or favorite toys, but after some time, even the favorites become boring. However, have you ever found an older toy in the basement that they forgot about or hadn't seen in a while? All of a sudden it is brand new again, and your kids are suddenly fighting over who gets to play with it first. Consider keeping different bins of toys and rotating through them. This way every couple days or weeks they have something new to play with.

There are also times when my kids would prefer to sit and make some artwork. Coloring can be very calming and therapeutic, and there are ways to help set them up so that you can use that quiet time as well. You can look into purchasing mess-free markers that only work on a certain type of paper. Or if your kids are ready for the responsibility, you can spread out a whole arrangement of coloring fun on the kitchen table. Baskets of markers, crayons, colored pencils, stencils, stickers, blank paper, and coloring books can provide great entertainment for kids.

Set Routines

Kids like to know what to expect, and it can help them to know that there is a concrete end in sight. If I have a work call, or if I need to block out a chunk of time to focus on something in particular, I will give them a time limit. "For the next hour, I need you to play quietly and only come to me if there is an emergency. If you can do this, then we can go outside and play." Now my kids know exactly what I expect of them, they have an end in sight, and I even offered something for them. I don't promise things like new toys or candy, because I'm really not asking that much of them. I'm simply asking them to play, not work, just play quietly. However, when the timer goes off, I am happy to spend some quality time with them to show my appreciation and encourage them to do a great job playing the next time I need to focus.

Creating simple routines and a sense of consistency can be very helpful for kids of all ages. If possible, I like to start the day with some energetic activity whether that means swim lessons or riding their bikes outside. Then right after lunch, I like to schedule some downtime. I'll separate the kids and assign them each to a specific room. If they are still taking naps, great! If not, establishing quiet time is wonderful too. The kids can play with toys, read books, draw, write, or even rest—it's up to them as long as they stay in their space and play quietly. This downtime allows all of us to take a break and recharge so that everyone can make it through the rest of the day with renewed energy.

Reasonable Consequences

To teach your kids anything new, they have to fully understand it. They need to know what their options are, what guidelines are in place, what is expected of them, and what happens if they don't follow those rules. When kids understand the boundaries, they are much more likely to cooperate. However, they are still kids. They need to hear things multiple times in several different ways. They will need practice—a lot of it! And they will be sure to test those boundaries to make sure that you really meant what you said.

When we hear the word "consequences," a lot of negative things come to mind. But that's not where we're coming from. Every action in this world naturally has an outcome. When we make good choices, there is a positive outcome. When we make poor choices, there is often a negative outcome. That is life. It is how things work in school, sports, jobs, and society as a whole. If we can help our kids learn this in a respectful way, they will be better prepared for their future.

When I need my kids to play independently for a while, there are certain expectations that come along with that. Since I have set up our home to be very kid-friendly, my kids have a lot of room to explore their independence and simply have fun. (Check out page 52 for some tips!) But I do expect my kids to play nicely with each other and their things. If they are being too rough with a toy, then that toy gets put in "time-out" for a certain amount of time—maybe an hour, maybe a week depending on what took place.

Another consequence that I implement is a group time-out. Recently, we had one of those afternoons where you could feel the tension rising. No one was doing anything that needed to be immediately addressed, but there was a lot of bickering and my gentle reminders to get along were not helping. So instead of letting it escalate further, I announced that they could either work it out amongst themselves, or I would be assigning them a group time-out. It didn't matter who was doing what . . . if I heard any more fussing, whining, or mean voices, then they were all going upstairs to their beds to lay quietly for fifteen minutes.

Guess what happened? It worked! All of a sudden the level of frustration coming from the playroom began to soften. I started hearing compromises like, "You can play with my toy if I can play with what you have." They found a way to all be in the same room and get along, which was amazing in and of itself. But the other benefit to this method is that if they hadn't turned their behavior around, I could have easily implemented a reasonable consequence. We always, always, always have to be ready to follow through on our word, and sending them all to their beds would have been totally doable in that moment if it came to that.

Explain the Importance of Your Work

Young toddlers might not understand what work is quite yet, but older children do. Explain what you are working on, and why it is important that you focus on that task. Oftentimes when my kids understand my goals and the reasons behind them, they become super supportive. I have had many talks with them about how loved they are, and how important they are to me and their dad, but they also know that our jobs are very important as well. We make it clear that even though our kids are our number one priority, we have to work in order to make money to pay for our house, our food, our clothes, their toys, and any activities that we want to do.

It can also help to tell your kids what you're working on. I make it a habit to ask my kids for their advice and input when I'm working on something that they show an interest in. I have gotten some genuinely helpful advice from my children, and they love feeling a part of things. When you wrap up something that you're especially proud of, show them and celebrate together! Just because your kids don't have jobs, doesn't mean they can't be supportive and happy for all that you do.

This isn't a one-time conversation. It is something that we discuss over and over as it comes up. And as the kids get older, they understand that when I'm on an important work call, it benefits the whole family if I can get through it in a professional manner.

As you are probably starting to realize, there is no quick fix for parenting children while working from home. It is all about opening up lines of communication, establishing reasonable guidelines, and working with your kids to find something that works great for the whole family. Day by day, you can start to increase expectations and decrease tensions within your home so that everyone has a happier experience.

*

Work from Home: Plan Ahead for the Holidays

Depending on the industry that you're in, December can either be really busy or really slow. Whether you are heading into a hectic few weeks, or you are trying to take some time off around the holidays, it's still important that you plan ahead for the holiday season.

With our parenting website, Adore Them, we put in a lot of overtime in the fall so that we can take it easy from Thanksgiving to the New Year. We make the effort to plan ahead, schedule out as much as we can, and set client deadlines before the holidays start. This means that we work like crazy during September, October, and the first few weeks of November so that we can take some time off while the kids are out of school and our holiday to-do lists are a mile long.

There will always be some things that we need to maintain through the upcoming weeks, and there is rarely a day that goes by that we don't have to fire up the computer, but at least our overall workload is much less than it would be without planning ahead.

Focus on the Basics

Whether this is your busy season or your slow season, it is beneficial to focus on the basics right now. What is the bare minimum that you need to do to keep things running smoothly? This doesn't necessarily mean that you will only do the bare minimum, but it is a good exercise to think through what has to happen, and what is optional.

Customer service always needs to be a priority—especially in this digital age. A bad review or two can make sales drop dramatically, which means that some form of pleasant customer service always has to be in place. You want to keep coworkers, clients, and customers happy; but you may be able to get creative with how you do that. You can set up auto-replies letting people know that response times may be a bit slower, create a list of FAQs to help you field some questions, or delegate this important task to someone who is looking for some extra seasonal income.

Sales and marketing is another basic element of any business. If you let those things slide, you won't feel the effects immediately; but you will notice a dip in sales a few weeks or months from now. You have to continually be adding people to your sales funnel through effective outreach and marketing so that your business stays strong in the future. (Visit AdoreThemParenting.

com/Book-Resources for a printable content calendar with a full year's worth of marketing inspiration.)

Think Ahead

While not everything can be done ahead of time, there are some aspects of your workload that can be accomplished now. Think through everything that your job requires, and make a list of items that you can work on right now. Do tasks in bulk to save time both now and when you want to take some vacation days. Minimize the phone calls and meetings that you agree to take in the weeks to come. Get started on year-end reports so that most of it is done when you get the final data. Create and schedule out a marketing campaign for the holiday season. All of those small tasks add up quickly! And you'll appreciate having less to do next month when you have a pile of presents waiting to be wrapped.

5 Things to Do before the Holidays

- Schedule email newsletters
- Create holiday graphics
- Schedule social media posts
- Update your website
- Schedule blog posts

Now is also the time to squeeze in last-minute business purchases before the end of the year. If you have been putting off certain buying decisions, it can be beneficial to move forward on those now—especially if you could use some extra tax deductions. You don't want to rush purchasing decisions or make them flippantly, but it is worth looking at and researching more thoroughly. And if you have something to sell, this can still be a valuable time to pitch your products and services to businesses! You may want to position this as a win-win if they are able to work with you before the end of the year and take advantage of tax benefits. Every situation is a bit different so you will have to figure out what makes the most sense for you and your potential customers, but it can be a great way to close out your year.

Spread Holiday Cheer

This time of year affects everyone differently. Some people are able to take more time off from now until the end of the year, while others are feeling swamped in the midst of a busy season. Either way, be patient with the people that you are working with. You will absolutely need to plan ahead because timelines are often extended throughout November and December. Don't expect quick responses from the people that you are working with, and don't expect your shipments to arrive or be delivered at their typical speed. If you treat everyone with an extra amount of patience throughout these next few months, they will appreciate it and be excited to work with you moving forward!

It is also your opportunity to spread a little extra holiday cheer to the people that you work with. Have your kids help you put together holiday cards to send to coworkers, clients, and customers. Offer holiday-themed giveaways, coupon codes, and little free surprises. Update your website to feel festive temporarily. Have fun with it . . . this only happens once a year!

Even CEOs take breaks, and so should you. No matter how busy your December is, you need to be able to take a mental break and unwind. Otherwise you will exhaust yourself, and your work will ultimately suffer. You deserve some downtime, and your family deserves it too. As much as you can, try to only focus on work when you are actually working. When you are spending quality time with your family, try to be present. Those boundaries are crucial to staying healthy and productive. They also help you to stay involved and tuned in with the ones you love.

The holidays go by so fast, and they offer the memories that children will carry with them throughout their lifetime. Yes, work is a critical part of our lives. There will always be things that you simply have to get done. But your kids likely won't remember how many deals you closed. They will remember if you were there to celebrate the holidays with them.

*

Monthly Reflections

Since parenting requires so much from us day after day, it can be hard to slow down and take the time to reflect on what's working and what we need to change. You might be tempted to breeze past these monthly checkpoints, but we highly recommend that you take a few minutes to stop and reflect on the past month while it's still fresh in your mind.

There are a few reasons to do this exercise each month. First of all, it encourages you to live and parent more mindfully. It is a checkpoint so that you don't continue on the same path month after month, year after year. If something isn't working well for you and your family, you have the opportunity to identify that and begin to correct it!

It also gives you the opportunity to highlight and appreciate the things that *are* going well. Feeling gratitude for amazing people and moments in your life will lead to even more positivity in the following month. We want to train our brains to see the bright side, and monthly reflections are a simple way to do that.

Once you work through your monthly reflections, you may want to share your thoughts with trusted loved ones in your life. It is a great way to share insight with your partner, your coworkers, and your friends. You can share new ideas with them, and they will be able to support you moving forward as well!

November
Monthly Reflections

Five Highlights
What were your favorite moments from the month?

_____

_____

_____

Four Things You Focused on
What took up the most brain power this month?

_____

_____

_____

Three Game Changers
What were those a-ha moments?

_____

_____

_____

Two Things You Didn't Get to
Do you need to get to them next month?

_____

_____

_____

One Disappointment
Did you take time to grieve that moment?

Next Month
What do you want to continue for the next month?

What do you want to change for the next month?

Notes

Chapter 12

December

December stands alone as a unique month for families when typical schedules go out the window. This chapter encourages you to slow down and find the magic in the holidays. We give practical tips for helping kids through this busy time without meltdowns. And we cover the importance of reflecting on your accomplishments and finishing out the year strong.

*

Monthly Intentions

At the beginning of each month, we'll leave space for you to prioritize, plan, and prepare. As parents, our lives can start to feel like a series of small emergencies. One simple way to keep things organized is to set clear priorities and plan accordingly for the month ahead. Answering these five questions at the start of each month only takes a few minutes, but it will help you feel organized and ready to tackle the next thirty days.

Note: Daily and weekly plans are a great way to make sure that you are maintaining your monthly priorities and staying focused. Free printable planners can also be found on our website: AdoreThemParenting.com/Book-Resources.

December
Monthly Intentions

1. What are some things that I can do to improve my own well-being?

_____

_____

_____

2. How can I support and connect with my partner?

_____

_____

_____

3. What do my kids need me to make a priority?

_____

_____

_____

4. What will I need to focus on for work?

_____

_____

_____

5. Which household tasks or projects need my attention?

_____

_____

_____

*

Focus on You: Find Magic in the Season

From November to January it feels like we are in the middle of a holiday-themed marathon. The lines can often become a little blurred as you fall asleep after celebrating one special event, only to wake up and embrace the next. Because there are only so many weekends to cram it all in, you may find yourself celebrating Thanksgiving one evening, and Christmas brunch the next morning with a different group of hosts. While it can be an exciting and invigorating time of the year, it can get exhausting and overwhelming at times.

This season can also bring with it a lot of hardship. While many of us are celebrating with loved ones in warm homes around dishes of tasty food, not everyone is as fortunate. Perhaps you too are dealing with family tensions, are in the middle of a health crisis, or have hit a financial rough patch. It can be gut-wrenching to try and pull anything together. And if you have kids, it's even harder to navigate through this time of year.

Having gone through some very personal struggles in the past around the holiday season, I know these feelings all too well. While I am happy to have made it through and to be on the other side of it, the memories and pain are still very raw at times, and the holidays can often amplify those emotions.

Embrace Change

While we want nothing more than to give our children the entire world, our kids are typically not expecting that. Oftentimes, kids don't really know what they are missing—especially if they are younger in age. When my family was going through our rough patches, we knew that we would not be getting together with the same people that we did in years past. This also meant that there wouldn't be as many presents under the tree. And since we were in the middle of a move on top of everything, there would not be as many holiday decorations, and we would not be celebrating in our old home.

There were so many difficult transitions in that phase of life, but instead of focusing on what we didn't have, we shifted our mindset and decided to make it an adventure. Kids pick up on what their parents are feeling so I was

168

determined not to be discouraging or negative in my mannerisms. Instead, I was motivated to make the best of our situation.

Our new little apartment had a real wood burning fireplace so we made it a point to enjoy this almost every winter night. We sold our large fake tree to have more room in the moving truck, but found the fun in picking out a cute, small tree that reminded us of Charlie Brown. We were still able to have cozy movie nights watching our favorite classics together. We played holiday music nonstop, and filled our little rental with the aromas of seasonal candles. And on Christmas morning there were still lots of laughs and giggles as the kids tore into their presents. They didn't know whether we spent more or less than last year, and they didn't care. The excitement was still magical.

And now a couple years later, we are living near the beach in the south. We have tried to create all new family traditions. We have swapped building snowmen for building sand sculptures at the beach. We drink our cups of hot cocoa on the front porch under our gas lanterns. We buy giant, fuzzy slippers that look silly with our shorts and T-shirts (because flannel is too hot to sleep in down here).

Of course I remember what things were like, and I know what is different now. But to my kids, they have really happy memories. They love reminiscing about our past Christmases in our old house. They love the memories from our tiny apartment where they all got to share a room. And they love what we have now. To them it was all wonderful, and it still is.

They feel loved. They feel safe. And they appreciate everything that we have, because we put an emphasis on being thankful instead of the "what-ifs" or the "I wants." We have everything that we need. We have each other, and that is what matters most. The rest is all just a bonus! And this life that we are living—it is filled with amazing adventures.

Find the Joy

The holidays are a lot of fun as an adult, but going through it as a child is a completely different experience! Having children allows us to experience it all a second time around through their eyes. It's like we are discovering the magic, the innocence, and the joy all over again. And the things that seem commonplace for us can be extra special to a child experiencing it for the first time.

So this year, no matter where you are in life, I encourage you to pause and appreciate all that you have. Take some time to reflect on your blessings, and what a privilege it is to end the year with your little family. Make sure to take a break from the chaos of the season, and enjoy all of those small magical moments. I too will be treasuring all of the holiday music, scented candles, cozy blankets, movie classics, delicious cookies, and amazing treats that my husband and kids love to create. And my wish for you is that this time of year will also be filled with much love, a lot of joy, and an endless amount of laughter.

*

Connect with Your Kids: Help Your Kids through the Holidays

Unfortunately, if your kid struggles with something at home, they won't magically be okay with it while you're at a holiday party. If they are a picky eater at home, they will be a picky eater at a dinner party. If they turn into a pumpkin at 8:00 p.m., they will start getting cranky around that time even at Grandma's house. If they are at the stage where they are struggling with separation anxiety, they certainly won't want to leave your side when a lot of people are around. There are things that we can do to help them through these situations and support them, but we also want to be realistic with our own expectations.

Practice Behavior

Opening and reacting to presents was something that my kids struggled with a bit. It was embarrassing as a parent to watch them open a gift from a loved one and blurt out, "I already have this," or even worse. I brought it up with my child's therapist while we were talking through potential holiday struggles, and she reminded me that we simply needed to talk about and actually practice that skill! I took the time to have the conversation with my kids first. They were old enough to understand the concepts of empathy, and how it could really hurt someone's feelings when you don't like the present that they gave you. We talked about the realities of getting presents that we don't always love, but that we can still appreciate the thought behind them. That still happens to us as adults too!

Once I felt like they understood the importance of being polite in these situations, we skipped to the fun part . . . opening silly presents for practice. I would put a pair of socks or a mixing spoon in a gift bag and hand it to a kid to open. The rules of the game were that you had to smile and say thank you in a nice way. You didn't have to lie and say that you loved it (although me snuggling a dish towel and acting as if I loved it made us all giggle). You simply had to react politely. My kids had a lot of fun practicing with this game, and our holiday parties went a lot smoother after that thanks to those few moments of fun!

Come Up with a Plan

Before hosting parties at our house, I like to have a family meeting where we talk about the expectations for the evening. I check with my kids and make sure that if there are precious toys that they don't want touched, they are hidden away. I go over that I expect them to be kind and polite to the other people and to play nicely with the other children. We also talk about house rules, and what they can do if a problem comes up. If another kid is doing something they aren't supposed to, then they can come tell me, and the adults will take care of it. It's not their job to tell other kids what to do.

Things also go much more smoothly when we take the time to talk through other potential concerns as well. What are you going to do when your aunt wants to hug you? What can you do if all of the noise is starting to bother you? If I am talking to another adult, what can you say to get my attention? You don't have to give your kids (especially your young kids) an entire lecture. But highlighting the quick bullet points of expectations can make a world of difference for everyone!

Holiday Meals

When we are at a get-together, my kids never want to stop playing and take the time to eat. On top of that, they are also picky eaters. Thankfully most of our holiday parties are pretty laid-back and flexible. It's not abnormal for the kids to run around while grabbing a few crackers here or there throughout the party. But since I know what to expect, I try to feed my kids a real meal before we leave the house. I'll have them sit down and get some nutritious food in their bellies so that I don't have to worry about them being hungry and cranky while we're there.

On the other hand, if the expectation is that the children should sit down and eat the holiday meal with the rest of the group, then you will need to adjust your plans accordingly. If they struggle with sitting still, you can practice this expectation leading up to the party. You can also compile a list of fun conversation starters or, my kids' personal favorite, "would you rather" questions that can help keep them entertained throughout the meal.

Conversation Starters for Kids

Visit our website for more mealtime resources for kids: AdoreThemParenting.com/Book-Resources.

1. What is your favorite thing to do in the winter?
2. What do you think winter is like in other parts of the world?
3. What is your favorite game to play inside?
4. What makes you feel happy?
5. What are you thankful for?
6. What is something that you really want to learn this year?
7. What do you want to be when you grow up?
8. What is something that you have in common with someone here?
9. What was your favorite vacation ever?
10. What is your favorite song to dance to?

Minimize Schedules

You might feel obligated to visit three houses in one day in order to see all of the relatives, but is that actually fun for anyone? Once you have your own family, you can set your own boundaries. What works one year, may not work the next—and that's okay. You can create new traditions and do what is best for you and your kids.

The fact of the matter is that kids get cranky when they get tired. And if you have kids at the ages where they still nap regularly, you might be able to get away with blowing through one nap time, but don't expect things to go smoothly on day two of no naps. While it can be frustrating to feel like you're missing out and having to schedule around your kids, please know that it won't last forever. A traditional New Year's party with a midnight ball drop might not be in the cards for this year, but pretty soon it'll be your kids trying to keep *you* awake to celebrate!

The whole goal of holiday festivities is to have fun, enjoy time together with loved ones, and celebrate the joys of the season. Do what you can to make that happen, while also being realistic about how much your family can handle in this phase of life. Don't dread this holiday season—make the most of it!

*

Work from Home: Finish the Year Strong

You've made it through another year! There were days when you felt like you were treading water, accomplishing nothing meaningful. And there were days when you felt like you were flying through your work with ease. This ebb and flow is totally normal, and we have to keep that top of mind as we head into a new year. We can't expect to have our act together every single day, but we can keep moving forward despite those rough phases.

Enjoy the Season

Don't feel like you have to do what everyone else is doing. Instead, tune back into you and your family throughout the month. Commit to unplugging as much as you can and make the effort to spend extra quality time with your loved ones. Make the effort to recharge so that you can head back to work feeling motivated in the new year.

It is also a fun time to enjoy your business as well! There is a festive spirit in the air, and many companies shift toward a more positive and personal tone throughout the holiday season. This provides you with a chance to flex those creative muscles and join in the fun. Keep things light, friendly, and don't be afraid to share the more heartfelt side of your work.

You can also get into the habit of spreading some holiday cheer each December. It is a great time to send out thoughtful thank-you notes to clients, surprise loyal customers, and extend warm wishes to your team. Try to brainstorm creative ways to provide extra support to your professional network as well.

Look Back on the Year

We often feel the need to keep rushing ahead, keep striving, and keep pushing. But this can accidentally hold us back. Taking the time to reflect on the work that got us to this point can help us build confidence, give us a sense of achievement, and inspire us to keep going. Throughout this book, we have encouraged you to take the time out of your busy schedule to work through the Monthly Intentions and Monthly Reflections. Those were building blocks that helped you get into the habit of looking at your life in a different way. We want you to take control of your life, and we want you to realize how much things can change when you make the effort to troubleshoot your recurring problems.

And while these monthly tools are very helpful in our personal and professional lives, it can be extremely rewarding to look back on the year as a whole. What were some of your top career achievements? Celebrate those wins! What did you learn? Commend yourself for coming so far! Where were you at professionally in January? Look how much you got done in the last twelve months!

Start Strategizing

You'll also want to analyze your year to figure out what worked and what did not work. Don't waste any time making old mistakes in the new year. And when you're reviewing your entire year at a glance, you might start to notice trends that you wouldn't have seen otherwise. Did you have a certain month that was significantly better than the others? Do you know why? Can you recreate that?

We also tend to get caught up in "best practices." We read an article telling us the "right" way to handle digital marketing, and then we get bogged down in the details of doing that thing. Don't get me wrong, digital marketing can be amazing! But it can also be a huge drain on your time. Make sure that you are doing things that actually get you results instead of blindly posting to social media or paying for services because you are "supposed to." Allow your reflections to result in actual change for you and your work.

On the other hand, you don't always have to reinvent the wheel. If you had a stellar year, then keep that going! Figure out how to build on that success. And if something is already working, just double down on it. As long as you are staying focused and keeping your priorities in order, then you will continue along the right path. You can take comfort in knowing that you are doing what is best for you and your career on any given day.

While working from home does merge our personal and professional lives, it can be beautiful. We can be an example to our children. We can show them firsthand how to manage time, advance in a career, and even show them the work that we do. It's bring your child to work day—every day! Which means they are there to give you breaks when needed and celebrate with you after a successful day "at the office."

*

Monthly Reflections

Since parenting requires so much from us day after day, it can be hard to slow down and take the time to reflect on what's working and what we need to change. You might be tempted to breeze past these monthly checkpoints, but we highly recommend that you take a few minutes to stop and reflect on the past month while it's still fresh in your mind.

There are a few reasons to do this exercise each month. First of all, it encourages you to live and parent more mindfully. It is a checkpoint so that you don't continue on the same path month after month, year after year. If something isn't working well for you and your family, you have the opportunity to identify that and begin to correct it!

It also gives you the opportunity to highlight and appreciate the things that *are* going well. Feeling gratitude for amazing people and moments in your life will lead to even more positivity in the following month. We want to train our brains to see the bright side, and monthly reflections are a simple way to do that.

Once you work through your monthly reflections, you may want to share your thoughts with trusted loved ones in your life. It is a great way to share insight with your partner, your coworkers, and your friends. You can share new ideas with them, and they will be able to support you moving forward as well!

December
Monthly Reflections

Five Highlights
What were your favorite moments from the month?

_____

_____

_____

Four Things You Focused on
What took up the most brain power this month?

_____

_____

_____

Three Game Changers
What were those a-ha moments?

_____

_____

_____

Two Things You Didn't Get to
Do you need to get to them next month?

_____

_____

_____

One Disappointment

Did you take time to grieve that moment?

_____

_____

_____

Next Month

What do you want to continue for the next month?

_____

_____

_____

What do you want to change for the next month?

_____

_____

_____

Notes

_____

_____

_____

_____

_____

_____

_____

_____

_____

Look Ahead

You've made it through another year; and you didn't just survive, you started to thrive! Our hope is that you have been able to establish a growth mindset throughout the course of this book. That you have realized that you can regain control of your life, your work, and your home. That by being purposeful in your communications and actions, you are able to make meaningful changes. And that you have the power to make things better for you, your family, and your career!

Before you dive into a whole new year, take the time to reflect on this past year. Sit down as a family and look through photos and videos. Enjoy seeing how much everyone has grown, the fun you had, and the things you learned together. Even though you likely had days when you felt like you were falling short, over the course of a year you managed to squeeze in a lot of amazing stuff!

It can be so rewarding to look back through the year and remember how much you accomplished. It felt like a lot because it *was* a lot! Scroll back through your email inbox for proof that you've fielded a lot of information throughout these last twelve months. Take credit for all that you've done and celebrate that. And remind yourself that the times when you came up short have probably been long forgotten.

No year will ever be perfect, but you've done a pretty incredible job balancing it all!

Year-End Reflections

Personal Development
What did you learn about yourself?

_____

_____

_____

What are some of your strengths?

_____

_____

_____

What continues to be difficult for you?

_____

_____

_____

Parenting
What tips did you implement in your own household?

_____

_____

_____

Have you stayed consistent with the things that work well?

_____

_____

_____

How have your family's needs changed throughout the year?

_____

_____

_____

Working from Home

What were some of your career highlights this year?

_____

_____

_____

What do you enjoy most about working from home?

_____

_____

_____

What is the most frustrating thing about working from home?

_____

_____

_____

New Year Intentions

Now that you've reflected on this past year, it's time to look ahead!

Personal Development

What areas of personal development do you want to work on?

_____

_____

_____

How will you carve out time for yourself this year?

_____

_____

_____

Parenting

What are some of the big family milestones ahead of you?

_____

_____

_____

How can you best support your family's unique needs?

_____

_____

_____

Working from Home

What are your goals as you look ahead to the next year?

_____

_____

_____

How can you troubleshoot your work-from-home frustrations?

_____

_____

_____

Start Over

The New Year gives us the chance to start over again, but this year, your starting point is well beyond what it was last year. You have learned so much, have had so many life experiences, and have stayed the course with your goals, which means that you will be approaching this next year with an entirely different perspective. You will be able to build on everything you have done up until this point. Even your mistakes are helpful in guiding you into the future.

This provides you with a great opportunity to loop back around to the beginning of this book so that you can pick up on things that didn't hit home for you the first time. Your kids will be older, you will have grown as a person, and you will be in a different place professionally. So we hope that you'll keep this book on your coffee table and revisit it throughout the upcoming year!

Join Us Online

If you have found this book helpful, we hope that you join us online as well! We have compiled free resources as a companion for this book at AdoreThemParenting.com/Book-Resources that are available at your convenience. We consistently share helpful parenting content through our website and email newsletter. And we love hearing new ideas and stories from fellow parents, so you are welcome to reach out to us anytime!

But more than anything . . . we want to say, "Thank You!" We put our hearts into this book, and it means the world to us that you have spent your valuable time reading it. Our mission is to help fellow parents find ways that will help them truly enjoy their family's journey, and we are so grateful that we've had the opportunity to share this book with you.

Sending you warm wishes and all our support,
Karissa & Shari

About the Authors

Shari Medini is a writer and co-owner of AdoreThemParenting.com. Her parenting articles have been published in dozens of print and online publications. Shari's past experience includes working with children and families in the mental health field, mentoring and speaking as a mindset coach, and working as a freelance writer and marketing strategist for companies across the country. She understands the demands of working from home and loves sharing tips to help balance it all. When she's not on her laptop, Shari can be found spending quality time with her husband and two sons exploring their hometown of Lancaster County, Pennsylvania.

Karissa Tunis is a writer, event organizer, and co-owner of AdoreThem Parenting.com. Through these ventures she has been able to share inspiring, heartfelt insight with large audiences both within local communities and across the country. As a work-from-home mom of four children, Karissa understands the need for family-focused organization and time management. She consistently provides insight into child behavior that has helped fellow parents achieve their goals of calmer, happier homes. Karissa also makes it a priority to soak in all of the southern specialties that Charleston, South Carolina, has to offer with her husband and their children.

Acknowledgments

The spring and summer of 2020 were unlike anything we could have expected. We faced constant changes and challenges while also being provided with the opportunity to make our dreams come true! We were able to make this book a reality in the midst of a pandemic, virtual schooling, having a new baby, and of course, working from home.

Thank you to Skyhorse Publishing for taking a chance on us and helping us share our first book with the world. Thank you to our editor, Nicole Mele, for walking us through each stage of this whirlwind of a process. And thank you to our agent, Keely Boeving, for seeing our potential and helping us find a home for this book.

Thank you to our support system for being there with a fresh perspective, kind words, and a dose of encouragement any time we needed it. Thank you to our husbands, Marcello and Scott, for all of your insight, understanding, and support! You both jumped in and held down the forts while we worked crazy hours to pull this together. And lastly, thank you to our kids—Matteo and Julian; Mady, Carter, Cohen, and Connor. You made us mamas, and we adore the moments that we get to spend with each of you!